*Elizabeth stands at the very centre of her realm. Her Majesty's radiant gaze disperses the storms to cast her kingdom in sunshine.*

RICHARD TAMES

# SHAKESPEARE'S LONDON
## ON FIVE GROATS
## A DAY

*with 82 illustrations, 16 in color*

# CONTENTS

VII

## MUST-SEE SIGHTS 88

VIII

## SHOPPING 99

IX

## CELEBRATIONS 115

X

## ENTERTAINMENT 122

XI

## AWAYDAYS 136

# I · PREPARING

*Background Reading · Purpose of Your Visit*
*History Today · Her Majesty*

WHEREVER YOU ARE FROM, DON'T expect Londoners to be impressed. They know their city in this year of Our Lord 1599 may not be the biggest in Europe – yet. They certainly think it the best.

*For the order of the city in manners and good fashions and courtesy, it excelleth all other cities and towns.*

ANDREW BOORDE · 1548

*No city in France is to be compared with it, first for the most pleasant situation; then consider ... the beautiful palaces, places and buildings royal ... the godly bringing up of youth and activity of their children to learning... the pleasant walks without every port for the recreation of the inhabitants.*

JOHN COKE · 1550

⊛⊛⊛⊛⊛⊛⊛⊛⊛⊛⊛⊛⊛⊛⊛⊛
⊛    **LONDON LANGUAGE**     ⊛
⊛    *Bedlam* – Bethlehem Hospital    ⊛
⊛       for the deranged       ⊛
⊛            ❧           ⊛
⊛      *port* – city gate      ⊛
⊛            ❧           ⊛
⊛ *quarantine* – isolation, from the ⊛
⊛    Italian quaranta = forty    ⊛
⊛            ❧           ⊛
⊛ *ward* – one of 26 areas into which ⊛
⊛   the City of London is divided for   ⊛
⊛      local administration      ⊛
⊛⊛⊛⊛⊛⊛⊛⊛⊛⊛⊛⊛⊛⊛⊛⊛

It will reassure you to know that quite a number of foreign visitors seem to agree:

*This city is rich in grocery, in cloth, linens, fisheries and has one of the most beautiful bridges in the world.*

STEPHEN PERLIN · 1550

*This city is great in itself but also has spacious suburbs and a magnificently built castle, called the Tower ... In London kings are crowned in style and inaugurated in splendid ceremonies ... It is a wonder for learned men.*

GEORG BRAUN AND FRANZ HOGENBERG · 1572

Be warned, however:

*The inhabitants ... are extremely proud and overbearing; and because the greater part, especially the tradespeople, seldom go into other countries but always remain in their houses in the city attending to their business, they care little for foreigners but scoff and laugh at them.*

FREDERICK, DUKE OF WÜRTTEMBERG · 1592

Yet if you are making London your prime destination you will be gratified by this particular up-to-date endorsement:

*London is ... so superior to other English towns that London is said not to be in England but rather England to be in London, for England's most resplendent objects may be seen in and around London: so that he*

*Hazards of the road. Unlike Macbeth you will probably not encounter three witches on the road to London – one maybe.*

*who sightsees London and the royal courts in its vicinity may assert without impertinence that he is properly acquainted with England.*

THOMAS PLATTER • 1599

## BACKGROUND READING

I F YOU ARE THE SORT OF TRAVELLER WHO likes to do your homework before you set off, there are some essential books to get hold of. Browse *Britannia* by William Camden for the definitive survey of the country's antiquities and monuments; only available in Latin, however. For history read Raphael Holinshed's *Chronicles*. These form part of an over-ambitious scheme dreamed up by the Queen's Printer Reginald Wolfe for a history of the entire world. Wolfe put 25 years into the project without actually getting anything into print. A consortium of publishers scaled it down after his death to concentrate on England, Scotland and Ireland. Unless you have a serious interest in ancient history you will only need Volume II, which covers the period since the Norman Conquest – in 1,876 pages. The revised second edition takes events up to 1586. William Shakespeare and others use the Chronicles as the major source for their historical dramas – sometimes line for line!

*Historian William Camden is also Headmaster of the prestigious Westminster School.*

As part of the revised Holinshed scheme the publishers commissioned the Reverend William Harrison to compile a contemporary *Description of England*. This is excellent, shrewdly observed, racily written and to be trusted, despite its occasional eccentricity. Devoting a whole chapter to the fierceness of English dogs seems a trifle too accommodating of this national obsession.

On London itself what must surely be the definitive account has just been published by John Stow. Unlike the other eminent authors noted above, Stow is not a university man but entirely self-educated. Trained as a master tailor, he has lived all his life in London and has personally witnessed the great changes that have so transformed it over the last 70 years. His appetite for collecting old books and pamphlets has brought him trouble with the authorities because many of these are from the days before the reformation of religion but, on examination, no one has doubted the author's patriotism. Stow's *Survay of London* covers the capital ward by ward in exhaustive detail. One can safely predict that this volume will never go out of print.

You will also need good maps. Mapping the country progresses constantly but slowly. Between 1575 and 1579 Christopher Saxton, with the authority of the Privy Council, produced the first ever set of maps of all the counties of England and Wales. Since 1593 John

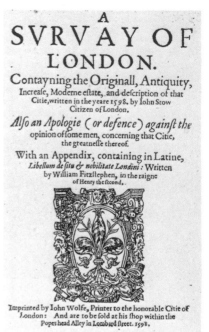

Imprinted by Iohn Wolfe, Printer to the honorable Citie of London: And are to be fold at his fhop within the Popes head Alley in Lombard ftreet. 1598.

*Stow's* Survay of London *includes William FitzStephen's account of London c. 1170 – the first ever description of London by a Londoner.*

Norden has been attempting to update them. So far he has proceeded largely at his own expense and seems unlikely to complete his self-appointed task in the near future. The visitor can, however, benefit from new Norden maps which are likely to be of most use to him, covering the counties around London – viz. Middlesex, Hertfordshire, Essex and Surrey.

## PURPOSE OF YOUR VISIT

SEEING LONDON NEEDS NO FURTHER justification. But if you have some other particular, practical purpose in mind, such as business, medical treatment, education or legal training, the following notes may be helpful.

## BUSINESS

*London is a large, excellent and mighty city of business and the most important in the whole kingdom: ships from France, the Netherlands, Sweden, Denmark, Hamburg and other Kingdoms, come almost up to the city, to which they convey goods and receive and take away others in exchange.*

FREDERICK, DUKE OF WÜRTTEMBERG • 1592

As one might expect of an aristocrat from a landlocked province far from

*One big city. Westminster, once the court suburb, is now joined to London by riverside residences, but the countryside is never far away.*

any coast, the Duke of Württemberg has failed to see how just far beyond Europe English commerce now reaches. Richard Hakluyt (pronounced Haklit – you'll just have to get used to the way the English pronounce their names) is the self-appointed chronicler of English 'stirrers abroad and searchers of the remote parts of the world' and modestly points out that 'in this most famous and fearless government of her Most Excellent Majesty, through the special assistance and blessing of God … they have excelled all the nations and people of the earth'. For the first time the English flag has been flown in the Caspian Sea and trading privileges have been negotiated with the Emperor of Persia, the Ottoman Sultan and the Princes of the Spice Islands. There are English agents

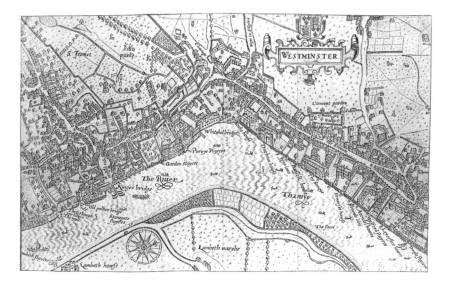

## GOLD COINS

| Name | Value in Shillings |
|---|---|
| Sovereign (23½ carat gold) | 30 |
| Sovereign (22 carat) | 20 ( = 1 pound) |
| Ryal / Rose Noble | . 15 |
| Half-pound / Angel | 10 |
| Half-angel / Angelet | 5 |
| Half-crown / Quarter Angel | 2½ |

## SILVER COINS

| Name | Value in Pence |
|---|---|
| Shilling | 12 |
| Sixpence / Tester | 6 |
| Groat | 4 |
| Threepence (say 'thruppence') | 3 |
| Half-Groat | 2 |
| One and a half penny | 1½ |
| Penny | 1 |
| Three-farthings | ¾ |
| Halfpenny (say 'haypnee') | ½ |

The English call their currency sterling, from Easterling, a compliment to the good-quality silver coins used for payment by merchants from eastern Europe. For a silver object to be labelled as sterling it must be at least 925 parts silver to 75 parts copper. The word has also passed into general speech so if someone calls you 'a sterling fellow' it doesn't mean he thinks you're a money-lender but a trustworthy person.

As a leading international port, London has a good deal of foreign coinage in circulation. Dutch florins exchange for 2 shillings. A Spanish ducat exchanges for 6 shillings and 8 pence – half a mark. A French crown may generally be reckoned to be worth 6 shillings or 6 shillings and 4 pence – you're never quite sure with the French.

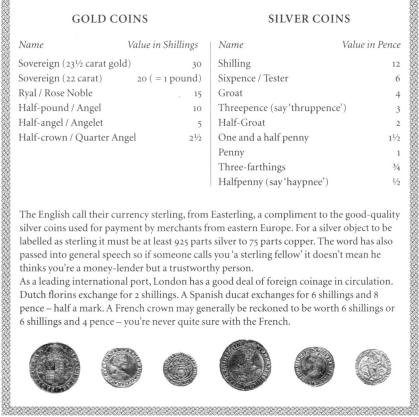

at Tripoli, Aleppo and Basra. English ships challenge the Portuguese in their Indian trading stronghold at Goa, anchor in the River Plate, 'range along the coast of Chile, Peru and all the backside of Nova Hispania … traverse the mighty breadth of the South Sea … and … return most richly laden with the commodities of China'.

For advice on markets and shopping please consult Chapter VII.

### MEDICINE

As a traveller in a foreign country you will be pleased to know that, in the unfortunate case of illness or accident, the best medical assistance can be found in London.

London's physicians stand at the apex of the profession and have, since 1518, been organized as a Royal College, empowered to regulate admission to their number and maintain standards of practice. Admission depends upon performance in examinations which are, naturally, taken in Latin and therefore inevitably exclude women. By an Act of Parliament the cadavers of four executed criminals are provided yearly for the purposes of anatomical lectures for students at the College. You may find it instructive, not to say diverting, to attend one of these sessions. A generous tip to the porter at the dissecting room should secure admission.

Physicians have a monopoly on prescribing all 'inward' medicines, whether in the form of liquids, pills or enemas. The prestige of London physicians means that they are very often consulted by letter and prescribe a course of treatment by correspondence, without actually examining or even seeing the patient.

Next in standing to physicians come the barber-surgeons, who have been united as a single corporate body since 1540. Their main concerns are bonesetting, bleeding and extracting teeth. They do also shave and cut hair.

Apothecaries are not yet organized as a corporate body but are growing in prestige. They are currently licensed by the Worshipful Company of Grocers which also controls the import trade in medicinal drugs. The apothecaries' main business is the preparation of medicines prescribed by physicians and the sale of the ingredients used in the preparation of home remedies. Herbalists are allowed to prescribe basic remedies for everyday ailments and afflictions. Many ply the streets, crying their trade and will accept payment in kind rather than cash, usually in the form of a meal or items of food.

Midwives are licensed by the Church. They are empowered to perform emergency baptisms, sworn not to perform abortions or use witchery and, in the absence of an evident father, they are obliged to try to discover his identity to prevent the child becoming a charge on the parish.

Most Londoners opt for self-medication in the first instance and are assisted in this by the proliferation of medical handbooks now available in English rather than Latin, a development most displeasing to the collegiate physicians.

## LONDON LIVING

After decades of debasements, the quality of English money has been fully restored. But no one seems to have taken the opportunity to cut down the number of different coins, several of which have more than one name. For everyday reckoning purposes you need to know that there are 12 pennies (pronounced pence) to the shilling and 12 shillings to the pound. There is also an accounting unit, called a mark, equal to 13 shillings and 4 pence (two-thirds of a pound) and often used for wages, pensions, rents and other business purposes. However, no coin equal in value to a mark exists.

*During an epidemic most corpses will be flung into a pit, rather than given a proper burial in a coffin.*

*The Breviary of Health*, compiled by Andrew Boorde, a former monk, has been a trusted authority for half a century. Most recently John Gerard has published a comprehensive *Herbal*, describing some 300 plants and their uses, including medical applications.

---

### PRECAUTIONS FOR PESTILENCE

Like every other major city London is subject to periodic visitations of the plague and other outbreaks of epidemic disease. The city's authorities follow the best current Italian practice in the enforcement of regulations to mitigate its impact, viz:

◆ Newly arrived ships are quarantined for 40 days.

◆ Afflicted houses are shut up with all their residents for 20 days.

◆ Theatre performances, fairs and other unnecessary public assemblies are banned.

◆ No more than six persons may attend a funeral.

◆ Persons recovering from infection must carry a yard-long white wand.

◆ All stray dogs and cats are killed and the keeping of swine within the city walls is forbidden.

◆ Bonfires are lit at street corners to purify the air.

◆ Beggars are driven from the city.

◆ The clothes and bedding of afflicted persons are burned.

◆ 'Viewers' are appointed to visit houses and confirm the cause of death.

◆ Pesthouses are opened on the fringes of the city for the reception of the dying.

Weekly plague deaths have been systematically recorded by parish clerks for over 40 years. The Worshipful

### LONDON LIVING

If – Heaven forbid! – you should by chance be wounded send for William Clowes, London's surgical supremo. Clowes has learned his trade by practical experience in the army and the navy, and by serving as surgeon to St Bartholomew's Hospital. He discovered on the battlefield that scabbards make excellent splints and has invented his own powder for staunching bloody wounds. He is an expert on syphilis and embalming and the author of *Proved Practice for Young Chirurgians Concerning Burnings with Gunpowder and Wounds Made with Gunshot, Sword, Halberd, Pike, Lance or Such Other.* He is Surgeon to the Queen. Need one say more?

Company of Stationers submits to the government an annual summary of the returns for the whole city, distinguishing plague deaths from others and identifying parishes free of infection.

The ancient hospitals of St Bartholomew and St Thomas are primarily intended for the treatment of London's poor, Bedlam for the reception of the deranged. In case of any more than minor illness, install yourself in a good inn with a couple of stout menservants. Send one for the best physician you can afford. If he refuses to take you into his own house until you are recovered your men can ensure, by payment if possible, by force if need be, that your wants are attended to.

### EDUCATION

You may be considering sending a son to London for his schooling, in which case there is an excellent choice available. All offer a solid grounding in Latin, whence they are called grammar schools. Most are free but boys may be expected to provide their own candles in winter and to pay a tip to the school's cleaners. Normal hours are 7 to 11 o'clock in the morning and 1 to 5 o'clock in the afternoon with Tuesday and Thursday afternoons off.

St Paul's is the largest grammar school in the country. The founder, John Colet, was the son of a fabulously wealthy Lord Mayor of London and the only one of his 22 children to survive, so inheriting the entire fortune. This he

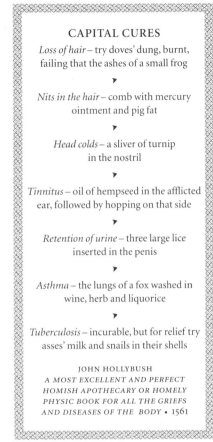

**CAPITAL CURES**

*Loss of hair* – try doves' dung, burnt, failing that the ashes of a small frog

*Nits in the hair* – comb with mercury ointment and pig fat

*Head colds* – a sliver of turnip in the nostril

*Tinnitus* – oil of hempseed in the afflicted ear, followed by hopping on that side

*Retention of urine* – three large lice inserted in the penis

*Asthma* – the lungs of a fox washed in wine, herb and liquorice

*Tuberculosis* – incurable, but for relief try asses' milk and snails in their shells

JOHN HOLLYBUSH
*A MOST EXCELLENT AND PERFECT HOMISH APOTHECARY OR HOMELY PHYSIC BOOK FOR ALL THE GRIEFS AND DISEASES OF THE BODY* • 1561

used to establish a school for 153 boys, the same as the number of fish caught in Our Lord's Miraculous Draught of Fishes. The school's statutes declare that pupils are to be 'of all nations and countries indifferently' and it is therefore particularly suitable for scholars from overseas.

The Queen herself re-founded the ancient school attached to Westminster

Abbey. Fee-paying pupils, known as 'town boys', are also admitted and there are 40 'Queen's scholars' who pay no fee. Westminster is noted for its annual Latin play which Her Majesty often attends. Pupils must speak Latin in school, not English.

Christ's Hospital was founded by King Edward VI in the former monastery of the Franciscans as a school for orphans. Girls are therefore also admitted. The boys may easily be known by their distinctive yellow stockings, which are said to keep rats away. (The city's main meat market and butcheries are just round the corner in Smithfield.) Music features prominently on this school's curriculum and the school has its own surgeon, barber and brewer. Most of the boys are apprenticed to trades and the girls become domestic servants.

Merchant Taylors' School emphasizes 'good manners and literature'. New pupils are expected to know the catechism of the Church of England. The school charges a sliding scale of standard fees, low fees and no fees, according to parental means.

Should you, or more likely your wife, be concerned about the risks of plague in the city – or the temptations of the city – there are several other free grammar schools within an hour or two's ride, as at Highgate, Barnet, Enfield, Harrow and Croydon. There are also a number of private schools run by individual masters, such as the Frenchman Claudius Hollyband's, in St Paul's Churchyard, and there are others for teaching accounts, business correspondence, languages etc.

Gresham's College, newly founded as an institution of higher learning, was established through the munificence of the late Sir Thomas Gresham, Her Majesty's confidential financial advisor. The seven professors lecture on Divinity, Rhetoric, Geometry, Medicine, Astronomy, Music and Law at Sir Thomas's former mansion on Bishopsgate.

*A teacher takes a top-class tutorial. Normally a class is a crowded schoolroom with dozens of boys of all ages.*

## LAW

Although law is taught at Oxford and Cambridge, those intending a professional career in the legal profession must train at one of the Inns of Court – Gray's Inn, Lincoln's Inn, Inner Temple and Middle Temple. Nine Inns of Chancery are attached to these, providing a preliminary training for pupils from the age of about 14 onwards. The Inns of Court resemble university colleges in being built around courtyards, enclosed from

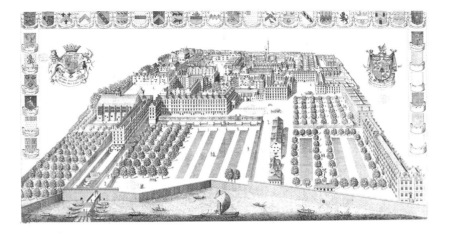

surrounding streets by gates and high walls, each with its own chapel, library, dining hall and gardens. Men aiming to practise law must study for seven years, attending lectures and mock-trials known as 'moots'. These latter are open to invited members of the interested public and you may wish to take advantage of this possibility as a source of free instruction – and entertainment. The English esteem wit – even, sometimes especially, in grave matters of property and crime.

Lord Burghley, the Queen's chief minister, Lord Howard, the Lord Admiral, Sir Walter Ralegh and Sir Francis Drake all spent time at the Inns of Court – but not to become lawyers. A large proportion, perhaps a majority, of the students at the Inns of Court stay for only one or two years. Oxford and Cambridge are losing their appeal for 'gentleman commoners' with no interest in actually taking a degree

*A garden city. Like the colleges of Oxford and Cambridge, the Inns of Court are renowned for their well-tended gardens.*

examination. They have no royal Court, no Royal Exchange, no theatres. A spell at the Inns of Court will, by contrast, enable a young man to polish himself by taking lessons from the very best teachers of music, dancing, fencing, riding etc., all of whom are in London. He can also make the sort of friends who will be useful to him in later life. And students are bound to pick up some smattering of law which will doubtless come in useful when they assume the responsibilities of gentlemen – quarrelling with neighbours over boundaries, disputing wills with their brothers and cousins and serving as magistrates to order the branding or flogging of vagrants, vagabonds, poachers and prostitutes.

*The power behind the throne: Lord Burghley, the Queen's most trusted advisor.*

## HISTORY TODAY

Shakespeare's historical plays have reminded a whole new generation of the English how their country was weakened and despoiled by discord before the present royal house restored its strength and reputation. To comprehend the universal reverence that Englishmen have for the Queen you must know a little of her immediate lineage and the character and achievements of her predecessors.

◆ **Henry VII** (1485–1509), the Queen's grandfather, gave the country a quarter of a century of peace after 30 years of civil strife. A brave warrior, he yet avoided wars, encouraged trade and left his successor a mountain of money. Faithful to his wife, pious before God, he was respected rather than loved.

◆ **Henry VIII** (1509–47), the Queen's father and her model of kingship, made himself head of the church, appropriated its lands and wealth, created the navy and owned over 50 palaces. The first monarch to be addressed as 'Majesty', he was in every respect larger than life and still casts a long shadow over this nation's memory.

◆ **Edward VI** (1547–53) the Queen's brother, a sickly, scholarly youth,

### LONDON LIVING

In 1589 William Darrell, a wealthy but quarrelsome West Country landowner, spent three months in London consulting daily with his lawyers about the dozen cases he was pursuing against various neighbours, tenants and relatives. Over that period his expenses were as follows:

|  | £ | s | d |
|---|---|---|---|
| Tips (to doormen, porters, carriers, beggars) |  | 14 | 1 |
| Washing |  | 17 | 5 |
| Boat Hire | 1 | 4 | 5 |
| Clothes and Mending | 4 | 3 | 1 |
| Sundries (tobacco, medicines, paper etc.) | 4 | 16 | 1 |
| Lodging (furniture, wages to cleaners etc.) | 12 | 11 | 7 |
| Travel (horse hire, feed, carriers etc.) | 21 | 18 | 0 |
| Food and Drink (self & four servants) | 42 | 6 | 10 |
| Living Expenses Total | 88 | 11 | 6 |
| Lawyers' Fees Total | 124 | 9 | 1 |

The price of justice!

introduced a Protestant prayer book in English as the standard form of worship and ordered the transformation of the nation's churches by removing all images and relics, whitewashing over paintings and abolishing the veneration of saints.

◆ **Mary** (1553–58) the Queen's sister, vainly attempted to re-establish the Roman faith, married Philip II, the king of Spain, lost Calais, England's last possession in France, and burned over 300 Protestants for their beliefs. The short, disastrous reign of this unhappy queen forms a most striking contrast to the long and glorious rule of her sister and successor.

*Happy families. Henry VIII is flanked by Queen Mary and her husband Philip of Spain (left) and by Queen Elizabeth (right).*

## HER MAJESTY

*Your Majesty and we your faithful and obedient subjects are but one body politic… no age either hath or can produce the like precedent of so much happiness under any prince's reign nor of so continual gracious care for our preservation as your Majesty hath showed in all your actions.*

PREAMBLE TO THE LARGEST GRANT OF TAXATION EVER GIVEN BY PARLIAMENT

*My mortal foe can no ways wish me a greater harm than England's hate; neither should death be less welcome unto me than such mishap betide me.*

ELIZABETH I

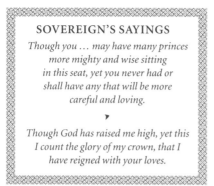

## SOVEREIGN'S SAYINGS

*Though you ... may have many princes more mighty and wise sitting in this seat, yet you never had or shall have any that will be more careful and loving.*

*Though God has raised me high, yet this I count the glory of my crown, that I have reigned with your loves.*

The glory of the Queen's Court shines not in Whitehall but in the minds of men. In every shire the Justices of the Peace serve as the workhorses of government. They see that the deserving poor do not starve, that church attendance is enforced, that vagabonds are whipped on their way, that roads are repaired and petty criminals are punished. These and many other duties they perform unpaid. But they do not do this for nothing, they do it for her. They are upholding 'The Queen's Peace'. On more than one occasion the Queen has reminded groups of these magistrates that as she must answer to God for the stewardship of her kingdom so they must answer to her for their care of her people – 'For they are my people.'

By general assent the greatest poem of the age is Edmund Spenser's *The Faerie Queene*, an immense epic of chivalric adventure written to glorify Her Majesty.

And she is, indeed, the Fairy Queen, because she has all England under her spell.

When she leaves her court she pauses at the door and surveys the assembled company – all on their knees – and, gesturing with her outstretched hand, sweeps over them with her eyes so that every single one feels sure that she looks only on them. The Queen never merely departs. She always makes an exit.

The Queen speaks Latin, Greek, French, Italian and Spanish fluently and can also understand Dutch, Welsh and Scottish. When she visited the University of Cambridge she was asked if she could say a sentence in Latin and made an impromptu speech of 600 words. When she visited Oxford she interrupted her Latin speech to ask in

*Best seller. Edmund Spenser's epic poem in praise of Elizabeth is the acknowledged masterpiece of our age.*

English for a chair for Lord Burghley, then resumed in Latin exactly where she had broken off.

*NO EASY THRONE*

The Queen has had anything but a charmed life. When she was still an infant her father had her mother, Anne Boleyn, executed on the grounds of her alleged adultery, which few have ever believed true. The Queen has never in her whole life ever mentioned her mother or so much as uttered her name. As a child Elizabeth was for years declared a bastard by law and excluded from the succession. As a princess she was imprisoned in the Tower by her own sister. She resisted every pressure to turn her from her Protestant faith but also avoided entanglement or even implication in any plot against the throne. By the time of her accession at the age of 25 she had acquired that iron self-discipline which underlies and underpins the dazzling brilliance of her reign.

*Portrait of power. The serpent on the sleeve of the Queen's dress is a symbol of royal wisdom.*

*SOUL OF THE NATION*

As 'Supreme Governor' of the Church of England the Queen has enforced a religious compromise which satisfies most of the people. The beliefs of the English Church are basically Protestant, but the outward forms of worship are in many ways still too Catholic for the extremists known as Puritans. Although Roman Catholics are penalized by fines and excluded from many positions of trust, they are not massacred as Protestants are in France.

Unlike her father, who squandered the nation's wealth in pursuit of military triumphs (to little effect), the Queen has always sought to avoid war or at least to keep it out of her kingdom, harassing her enemies in the Netherlands, in Ireland or on the high seas.

> **LONDON LORE**
>
> In 1579 John Stubbs published a pamphlet criticizing the Queen's proposed marriage to the Duke of Anjou. This impertinence cost Stubbs his right hand. When it was cut off he raised his cap with the left hand and cried, 'God save the Queen!'

When Spain sent its mighty Armada to invade England in 1588 the entire nation rallied to her and, as the inscription on the commemorative victory medal proclaimed, 'God Blew and They Were Scattered'.

## TUDOR TRADEMARKS

The royal house traces its descent from Wales and the royal colours of red, white and green are those of the Welsh flag. These are used on everything from tents and pavilions to the boards lining raised flower-beds in palace gardens.

⟩

To emphasize his ancient lineage Henry VII named his first-born Arthur, after the legendary King Arthur, whom he claimed as an ancestor.

⟩

The double rose of red and white, used both as a badge and a decorative device, symbolizes the reconciliation of the House of Lancaster (red) and the House of York (white) achieved by Henry VII in ending the Wars of the Roses.

⟩

The Welsh dragon features in much of the heraldic decoration of the royal palaces. Coincidentally the Spaniards call Sir Francis Drake, who has plundered many a Spanish treasure-ship, El Draque – the Dragon.

⟩

The Queen jealously guards her image as well as her appearance. Tavern signs depicting her can only use the official portrait approved by her Serjeant-Painter.

*A ROYAL PROGRESS*

If you want to get some idea of the place of the Queen in the hearts of the English people, take the trouble to find out from someone in the Lord Steward's department the route of her next intended summer 'progress'. With luck it will initially pass through some prosperous market town of note not too far from London, such as St Albans or Chelmsford or Farnham, where you can put up for a few nights and observe the frantic preparations for her passage through it. Every eyesore that can be removed – dunghill, gallows, stocks or pillory – will vanish. Houses and taverns will be whitewashed. The approach road will be gravelled, stages and arches erected. While the townsfolk dress their community for her reception, the mayor and council will debate the most suitable gift to offer Her Majesty and who best to deliver the oration being prepared by the schoolmaster. Should it be in Latin – or English? If she intends to arrive in the morning is there any point in ordering fireworks? Is the church choir really up to singing an antiphon? As the great day approaches habitual drunks, tarts, cripples and idiots will be rounded up by the constables and consigned to the lock-up, or, if too many, to the barn of a nearby farm.

When the Queen does arrive she will, as ever, astonish her entourage by the patience with which she sits through mumbled speeches, the good humour with which she applauds clownish

*The Armada Medallion recalls God's aid to the outnumbered English.*

entertainments, the graciousness of her offering of alms to the poor, the seeming intimacy and sudden gravity of her conference with the mayor and the aldermen, and the compliments she pays to their new market cross or grammar school. She might do anything – even enter a common tavern to sample the ale or the house of a widow to eat a slice of her locally renowned spice cake. And when she has gone the cup that she drank from will become a sacred relic and the room where she sat preserved as a shrine.

Why does she do it? Of course, to demonstrate her love for her people. But, more important, to tell them that they love her and that their love is 'of such kind as has never been known or heard of in the memory of man … such a love as neither persuasion, nor threats, nor curses can destroy.' She appears to halt and falter with emotion as she speaks, almost to weep. The people do weep.

There are also sound practical reasons for these progresses.

◆ First, any town she chooses to pass through will attract visitors from all the surrounding areas, thus boosting trade.

◆ Secondly, by accepting the lavish hospitality of grandees along her route she greatly diminishes her own expenses.

◆ Thirdly, London is at its least healthy in high summer and best avoided.

Organizing a royal progress really is like a military operation. The Queen must have not only her clothes and jewels, her books and her bed linen and her own barrel of specially brewed royal light ale, but also the wherewithal to transform anywhere she stays overnight into a royal apartment – so her hangings, furniture and plate. And government must be carried on, so piles of documents. And tents for those who cannot be found apartments. And blankets for those who sleep under the carts. In all 1,500 people move with her, requiring 400 carts and six times that number of packhorses. At most they cover 12 miles a day. They move every two or three days, having eaten like a horde of locusts.

On occasion the Queen stops at one of the many rural residences inherited from her father. Woodstock, outside Oxford, is unlikely: not much more than a hunting lodge and a place of unhappy memory where she was held in custody as a teenager. But there is also East-hampstead in Berkshire, New Hall in

---

### CAPITAL CURIOSITY

For writing *A Defence of the Seven Sacraments*, which upheld Catholic orthodoxy against the attacks of the German preacher Martin Luther, the Pope awarded Henry VIII the title of Fidei Defensor – Defender of the Faith. This title is still maintained by the present Queen – as a Protestant.

## LONDON LORE

When the Queen stayed with Sir Thomas Gresham at his house at Osterley she found fault with the courtyard 'as too great, affirming that it would appear more handsome if divided with a wall in the middle. What doth Sir Thomas but in the night time sends for workmen to London (money commands all things) who do speedily and silently apply their business, that the next morning discovered the court double, which the night had left single before.'

Essex, Oatlands in Surrey, where the hunting is excellent, and Hatfield in Hertfordshire, where she received news of her accession and held her first Council meeting. Mostly, however, she stays with those who can afford to entertain her in the style to which she feels entitled, a privilege liable to cost up to £1,000 a day. It is, however, the privilege of a lifetime – though not, perhaps, to be wished for twice in a lifetime.

### GOD SAVE THE QUEEN!

The Queen is in peril every day. Ever since she was excommunicated by the Pope for refusing to acknowledge his authority over the church in England it has been lawful for any Catholic to assassinate her with a clear conscience.

But even the Pope once said that if he could marry her their child would rule the world. To protect her from plotters Sir Francis Walsingham has created the most efficient espionage service in all Europe. A famous portrait of the Queen shows her dress embroidered all over with eyes and ears. The French ambassador De Maisse has paid tribute to her as 'a great prince, whom nothing escapes'.

The Queen has taken for her motto *semper eadem* ('ever the same') and so she strives to be. Having now ruled for 40 years she is the only sovereign most of her people have ever known. All of us are subjects of the Kingdom of Death, but when the English say 'May the Queen Live For Ever!' they mean it.

### GREATNESS FORESEEN

Archbishop Cranmer baptizes Elizabeth:
*This royal infant – heaven still*
*move about her! –*
*Though in her cradle, yet now promises*
*Upon this land a thousand blessings,*
*Which time shall bring to ripeness ...*
*She shall be, to the happiness of England,*
*An aged princess; many days shall see her,*
*And yet no day without a deed to crown it.*
*Would that I had known no more!*
*But she must die*
*She must, the saints must have her,*
*– yet a virgin,*
*A most unspotted lily shall she pass*
*To the ground, and all the world shall*
*mourn her.*

WILLIAM SHAKESPEARE • *HENRY VIII*

So, one final, absolutely crucial thing to remember – never, on any occasion, in any place, in any company, if you value your life, never, ever, say a word against the Queen.

# II · GETTING THERE

*Travelling by Sea · The Queen's Highway*
*Seasons & Weather · Where to Stay · That Language!*

## TRAVELLING BY SEA

**B**EING ON A SHIP IS LIKE BEING IN prison, with the additional possibility of being drowned. Travellers to England are advised to keep their journey as short as possible, which means crossing 'The Narrow Seas' between Calais or Boulogne and Dover. With a fair, following wind it is possible to do the journey in three or four hours, but even the most resolute of captains cannot bid the wind. So expect to depart when you can, not when you want. You may have to wait days or even weeks to make your crossing.

Most passengers have to seek what shelter they can on deck, but a share of a cabin can be bought at a price. One new comfort, brought in by the Spanish, is called a *hammacko*. This is like a shroud with strings at either end that can be slung from the ship's beams below decks, allowing a person to climb in and sleep. It is more comfortable than it looks, but climbing into it requires some persistence in all but the calmest of seas.

*They are good sailors and better pirates, cunning, treacherous and thievish; above three hundred are said to be hanged annually at London.*

PAUL HENTZNER
*TRAVELS IN ENGLAND* • 1598

If, when you do cross, the weather looks set to continue fair, you may wish to sail on round the coast and up the estuary of the Thames, either to Gravesend in Kent, from where you may proceed to London by road, or right into the city itself. The Lord Mayor is also Admiral of the Port of London, and, as such, wields authority over the Thames between Windsor and Gravesend. He appoints eight overseers to enforce the regulations governing river traffic.

There is also the possibility of travelling the last stage, starting at Gravesend, by public barge, which is slow but cheap. One precaution – literally take a good sniff before you board to ensure that your barge is 'sweet'. Many barges make their outward trip from London

[23]

carrying the contents of cesspits, to be spread on the market gardens on either side of the Thames estuary.

## THE QUEEN'S HIGHWAY

IN ENGLAND ROADS ARE NOT MADE – they happen, whenever a sufficient number of people and horses tread out a track to wherever they wish to go. The road from Dover to London is normally passable, but the routes to the capital from other main ports of arrival – Ipswich, Harwich and Southampton – do not compare well. The major highways between London and Plymouth, Chester and York are likewise passable in all but the worst winter weather. Regions of heavy clay soil, however, render the movement of wheeled vehicles virtually impossible for half the year. This applies particularly to the counties north of London, those to the south being mostly made of chalk.

Legally speaking each parish has a responsibility for road maintenance. By law all able-bodied men should work six days a year, eight hours a day on repairing the roads, an obligation widely evaded. Mending a through-route mainly benefits strangers, so if local residents do make a serious effort to repair a road it will most likely be a by-way leading to a field, a pond, a quarry or some other local place that matters to them, not to the traveller.

A fit man in fair weather might ride 60 or 70 miles in a day, as royal couriers do. The couriers, however, wear a distinctive

### LONDON LANGUAGE

*ale-conner* – official appointed to test the quality of ale and beer on sale to the public; Shakespeare's father once served as ale-conner in Stratford-upon-Avon

▸

*black-jacks* – leather bottles, used in alehouses and by travellers

▸

*livery* – distinctive uniform

▸

*stalling-ken* – premises where stolen goods are received

livery, which warns any ordinary rogue that they are under royal protection. For anyone not on official business such speed would be purchased at the expense of safety, a single rider being very vulnerable to ambush. Robbers hesitate to attack large groups riding in company, but these will inevitably travel much more slowly than a single man going 'post haste'.

*Safe voyage! English ships are sturdy but don't expect comfort.*

A royal courier might post from London to Edinburgh in five days; a normal traveller should reckon on taking three times as long. The 70 miles between Dover and London should take two days for the ordinary traveller, one for a strong man riding flat out. Completing the journey in one day, rather than two, will save the expense of a night's stay at an inn. Many travellers will not stop for dinner at midday, not so much to save money but so that they may be off the road well before nightfall and all its perils.

An ordinary riding-horse may be hired for days or weeks at the rate of 2 shillings for the first day and 18 pence or a shilling per day thereafter, plus the cost of its feed. This might be as much as another 12 pence overnight if the horse must be stall-fed, but if it can be turned into a field for grazing in summer, should be only 3 pence.

Carriers' wagons ply the roads between every market town. They are heavy, lumbering vehicles that move at little more than walking pace. But they give passengers shelter from the weather and are much used by single women in need of protection, the sick, the aged and the crippled. A traveller might find it useful to go himself on horseback but have a heavy trunk follow him on by wagon, to be collected at a London inn.

Regular weekly wagon services run between London and such towns as Oxford, Norwich and Chester. Packhorses are used by merchants for the transportation of non-perishables of reasonable value, such as books, pewter goods or bolts of cloth. Coaches are still a rarity in England and can be hired only in London. A coach and driver and two horses will cost 10 shillings per day. None will agree to go more than two days' distance from the capital, the ways

*Get your coachman to use his lash if beggars approach your carriage too closely.*

beyond that being so foul. Coaches are very slow and jolt the passengers badly, but may justify their expense for travellers that are very old or very young or burdened with much baggage.

## SEASONS & WEATHER

*Some by a painful elbow, hip or knee, Will shrewdly guess, what weather's like to be:*
*Some by their corns are wondrous weather-wise,*
*And some by biting of lice, fleas or flies;*
*For though these things converse not with the stars,*
*Yet to man's grief they are Astronomers.*

TRADITIONAL FOLKLORE

The English talk constantly of their weather because it changes constantly. Summers are often short and very wet. Winters can be savage. London, normally better favoured than the wild districts of the west and north of the country, can still suffer extremes of weather and rapid changes in a single day. So, if you are arriving from sunnier climes, keep a good, thick cloak where you can get it quickly. In 1565 and again in 1595 the Thames froze solid. In 1568 violent storms sank ships off Gravesend. In 1577, 2 ft of snow fell on the city. In 1589 there was an earthquake. Terrible summers every year between 1594 and 1597 caused the worst harvests in living memory. This led to famine in the remoter parts of the realm and, in 1595, to food riots in London itself, causing the Queen to declare martial law throughout the capital. Londoners were, however, spared from starvation because the city was wealthy enough to import grain from the Baltic countries.

*Which is the way to London town?*
*One foot up, the other foot down,*
*That is the way to London town.*

TRADITIONAL SONG

The English believe that severe weather is on its way if bees refuse to leave their hive, if cows and dogs are lying on their right side, if earthworms come to the surface or finches and sparrows chirp at dawn. Farming folk, whose living can literally be destroyed by frost, flood or hail, are

## LONDON LIVING

In 1582 Pope Gregory XIII introduced a new calendar which he claimed to be more accurate than the old one devised by Julius Caesar. This meant that Catholic Europe went to bed on 5 October and woke up the next morning on 15 October. England has declined to adopt the Gregorian system from popish Europe. Be aware of this when dating letters and especially when drawing up contracts or legally binding documents of any sort. Also the New Year begins in England on 25 March – but in Scotland on 1 January.

better attuned to weather warnings, but many Londoners are themselves newly arrived from the country and from long habit will note the colour of the sky, the movement of clouds, the way birds fly and the order in which plants open their leaves in spring, to be forewarned of the weather to come.

## WHERE TO STAY

### ALEHOUSES

If refreshment and occasionally rowdy company are all you want, alehouses and taverns will do. For somewhere to stay for the duration of your trip, however, you'll need to find a suitable inn, probably in Southwark (see below).

Alehouses are numerous, small and generally none too clean, though this may not matter to you since they do not normally let rooms overnight. As their name suggests they sell ale, usually brewed by the proprietor, who is often a woman. This is not, however, to be taken as an indication of the privileged status of the fairer sex in England. Widows are often allowed to keep an alehouse so that they can support themselves, rather than applying to the parish for charity.

An alehouse may also supply simple fare, such as bread, cheese or a pottage of beans with bacon. But don't look for a gourmet experience. It is an offence to drink in an alehouse during the hours of divine service on the Sabbath – but it is an offence committed by

*Eating at the common board requires you to make conversation.*

many except where Puritan zealots have taken control of a parish. If you're a Sunday drinker you'll find plenty of obliging outlets outside the city limits (see Chapter XI).

Just like a tavern or an inn, an alehouse must be licensed by a magistrate to prevent, in the words of Parliament, 'hurts and troubles ... abuses and disorders'. The proprietor also has to submit to having the quality of its ale tested by the ale-conner, and the price set by a local magistrate. Alehouses usually draw their custom from their immediate locality. In the worst parts of London, as at Wapping or Rotherhithe, there is an alehouse for every 20 households.

> *Of all in England there are no worse inns than in London, and yet many are there far better than the best that I have heard of in any foreign country ... Each owner ... contendeth with other for goodness of entertainment of their guests, as about fineness and change of linen, furniture or bedding, beauty of rooms, service at the table, costliness of plate, strength of drink, variety of wines, or well using of horses.*
>
> WILLIAM HARRISON
> DESCRIPTION OF ENGLAND

---

### TAVERNS

A tavern is considerably larger than an alehouse, sells wine as well as beer, and is run by a publican with a staff to help him to serve customers. Taverns are also places of amusement, where one may hear a harper or a ballad-singer, play at shove-penny, cards, dice or tables, or meet women who are no better than they ought to be. If you are short of a groat or two, tavern-keepers often have a sideline as lenders of small sums of money, but they are not the most reputable of people, and are widely suspected of accepting stolen goods in exchange for drink. Taverns don't usually offer rooms – except sometimes by the hour! If you are offered lodgings the tavern-keeper might have taken mercy on you as a stranger – or might plan to have you at his mercy. Best to smile and say you're already expected elsewhere.

---

### INNS

Inns are grand establishments, primarily intended for the service of travellers. The High Road of Southwark, leading up to London Bridge, is lined almost continuously on both sides with large inns. Some can accommodate up to 100 guests, with stabling for as many horses. The innkeeper himself is a person of considerable consequence in the community. In London they are organized as the Worshipful Company of Innholders, whose charter dates from 1514. English custom makes the innkeeper personally liable for the safety of his guests' goods while they are on his premises. Guests are allowed to lock their room and carry the key away with them.

Standards of service are high. On arrival a traveller is welcomed warmly and supplied with food and drink within minutes. In winter there is a roaring fire and wet clothes and muddy boots are whisked away to be dried out and brushed off. The traveller's horse is rubbed down and well fed. Guests can be confident of spotless sheets 'wherein no man hath been lodged since they came from the laundress'.

To eat at a common table at an inn might cost 6 pence for a basic set meal of meat, cheese, bread and beer. But you will be expected to join in the conversation, so be prepared for a possibly rowdy test of your grasp of English. To eat in the quiet of one's own room a meal of one's own choosing will cost four times as much. It is quite acceptable to set aside part of one's supper to be eaten as breakfast the following morning.

*Posthumous poet. Sir Philip Sidney's immense pastoral romance,* Arcadia, *has only been published since his tragic early death in battle.*

## THAT LANGUAGE!

Englishmen have sailed right round the world, but the English language has yet to leave these islands. Fortunately for the visitor, Latin and French are well and widely spoken, at least among the educated classes. In this the Queen herself has set an admirable example. Even the women of the court are expected to be fluent in French. According to William Harrison, 'the stranger that entereth into the court of England upon the sudden shall rather imagine himself to come into some public school of the universities, than into a prince's palace'.

Although no man can call himself educated unless he has at least Latin and French, there is a new pride among all classes in the English language. According to Sir Philip Sidney, 'for the uttering sweetly and properly the conceit of the mind, which is the end of speech ... English hath equally with any other tongue in the world'. Many learned men, who could publish their works in Latin to reach an international readership, now deliberately choose English to communicate as broadly as possible with their own countrymen. Books are being published simply about English as a language, such as Richard Carew's *An Epistle on the Excellency of the*

*English Tongue* and Thomas Wilson's *The Art of Rhetoric*. In an age when one may attain both fame and fortune as a preacher, a pleader or a poet, one should not, perhaps, be surprised.

## COURT SPEECH – CORRECT SPEECH

There is now a conscious concern and what one might call a national debate about what constitutes 'correct speech'. One school of thinking deplores the overuse of borrowed words, especially Latinate terms, as Roger Ascham argued in the preface to his landmark treatise on archery, *Toxophilus*: 'He that will write well in any tongue must follow this counsel of Aristotle, to speak as the common people do, to think as wise men do. Many English writers have not done so, but using strange words as Latin, French and Italian, do make all things dark and hard.'

George Puttenham, the learned author of *The Art of English Poesie*, likewise condemns what he calls 'inkhorn terms', 'brought in by men of learning, as preachers and schoolmasters; and many strange terms of other languages … daily spoken in court'. Whatever his reservations about courtly speech, however, Puttenham still looks to it as the proper standard, preferring 'that which is spoken in the King's Court or in good towns and cities … than in the marches and frontiers, or in port towns, where strangers haunt … or yet in Universities where scholars use much peevish affectation'.

## HAZARDS OF SPELLING

So at least a standard of speech exists to which the would-be learner can aspire and approximate. Regrettably, though there are books of grammar, the rules seem to be frequently ignored. Almost any word can seemingly be used as any part of speech, notably nouns as verbs. There is, moreover, as yet no definitive dictionary of English words. Fortunately, however, the English–French phrasebook published by William Caxton over a century ago is still being reprinted, and has been expanded to encompass Flemish, Italian and German. John Florio, an Italian of English birth and upbringing, has just published an Italian–English dictionary.

Spelling is a nightmare. Pedants have been busy adding letters to words – which no one pronounces – to make them more 'correct' in terms of their supposed origin. Hence the silent 'b' in doubt and debt, the 'p' in receipt and the 'c' in victuals, which is pronounced 'vittles'.

The names of places and persons constitute another endless hazard and source of potential embarrassment. Gloucester is pronounced 'Gloster' and Leicester, 'Lester'. Happisburgh, a village on the coast of Norfolk, is pronounced 'Hayzborough'. 'Cowpen' in Northumberland is 'Coopen'.

The English started using second names over 400 years ago but still haven't worked out how they should spell them. Even a prominent literary figure like Shakespeare fails to spell his own name consistently. But perhaps we should blame his father rather than Shakespeare himself. Town records at Shakespeare's birthplace show that his father, John, used 16 different spellings, most commonly Shaxpeare. The playwright himself has used Shakspere, Shakspeare, Shakespeare and, on legal documents, abbreviated forms like Shaxper, Shakp and Shaks. You can see the possible complications of all this in relation to disputed business dealings. And don't think his unusual name helps that much because it isn't unusual. There are records of Shakespeares now alive in 24 villages and towns of his native county of Warwickshire alone, and at least three of them are called William.

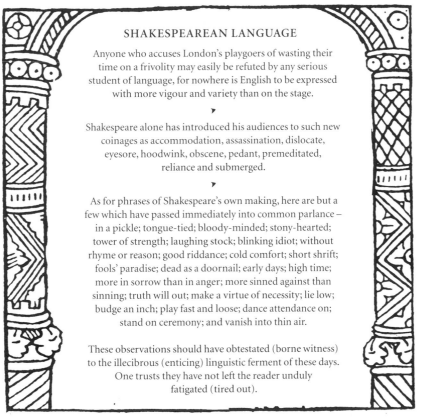

### SHAKESPEAREAN LANGUAGE

Anyone who accuses London's playgoers of wasting their time on a frivolity may easily be refuted by any serious student of language, for nowhere is English to be expressed with more vigour and variety than on the stage.

Shakespeare alone has introduced his audiences to such new coinages as accommodation, assassination, dislocate, eyesore, hoodwink, obscene, pedant, premeditated, reliance and submerged.

As for phrases of Shakespeare's own making, here are but a few which have passed immediately into common parlance – in a pickle; tongue-tied; bloody-minded; stony-hearted; tower of strength; laughing stock; blinking idiot; without rhyme or reason; good riddance; cold comfort; short shrift; fools' paradise; dead as a doornail; early days; high time; more in sorrow than in anger; more sinned against than sinning; truth will out; make a virtue of necessity; lie low; budge an inch; play fast and loose; dance attendance on; stand on ceremony; and vanish into thin air.

These observations should have obtestated (borne witness) to the illecibrous (enticing) linguistic ferment of these days. One trusts they have not left the reader unduly fatigated (tired out).

## A TONGUE WITH A MIGHTY MOUTH

Anyone who would set himself to master the English language must realize that it is a greedy monster, devouring new words every day, so that an Englishman's grandfather might struggle to understand him. Consider some of the words which have but recently been adopted into everyday speech.

From Latin – agile, genius, habitual, militia, reciprocal, inflate, defunct, spurious, strenuous and retrograde. From Greek – lexicon, chronology, catastrophe, rhapsody, phrase and pathos. Fighting the French has made the English familiar with such terms as machine, volunteer, battalion, cordon, cache, comrade, duel and bayonet and, less confrontationally, fricassee, genteel, vogue, portmanteau and moustache. English dealings with the Spanish have been likewise mostly commercial or bellicose – hence the adoption of such terms as cask, cargo, galleon, embargo, parade, flotilla, armada, tornado, renegade and desperado. There are also a few culinary borrowings, as in sherry, anchovy and rusk. Maritime links are particularly self-evident in borrowings from the Dutch – jib, keel, yacht, sloop, schooner, deck, dock, block, boom, splice, smuggle, skipper, cruise, reef and firkin. In culture and the arts Italy is most admired and influential. The technical terminology of both painting and architecture are both largely Italian in origin, as in cameo, studio, fresco, stucco, portico, balcony, cupola, cornice, corridor, colonnade, arcade, vista, villa, portfolio, piazza, parapet and design. Music is likewise in debt to Italian for violin, solo, aria, sonata, opera, fugue, madrigal, cantata and concert. Less friendly forms of contact have taught the English the meaning of squadron, salvo, frigate, escort, musket, stiletto, contraband and bandit.

It is noteworthy that, with the exception of whisky from Gaelic and penguin from Welsh, there are very few words the English have adopted from the languages of their neighbours in these islands.

New fields of learning also necessitate new terms, either to fix the meaning of what is newly discovered or to describe what is already known with greater accuracy. Of nothing is this more true than science and medicine. Hence the appearance of such words as explain, external, paradox, capsule, cylinder, prism, theory, energy, electric, system, larynx, thermometer, gravity, complex, radius, species, atmosphere, pneumonia, skeleton and excrement.

# III · LONDONERS

*A London Day · Londoners Proper*
*First Citizen · Homes · Gardens*

## A LONDON DAY

IF YOU CAN'T SETTLE TO SLEEP AS USUAL and find yourself up before the break of day, you may care to venture outside the city where the dust on the roads is already being stirred up by country higglers, burdened with baskets of eggs, herbs, flowers, butter and beans. As they pass by, the unlicensed beggars from the hedgerows are gathering their tatters and trying to bear themselves like honest men as they think how to slip through the city gates, past weary watchmen, to ply their trade on the streets of the capital. From time to time these figures, variously striding, shuffling or stumbling in the gloom, yield the road to lumbering country carts, packed with root vegetables, crates of live chickens, bundles of firing

*There squeaks a cart wheel,*
*Here a tumbrel rumbles,*
*Here scolds an old bawd,*
*There a porter grumbles.*

EDWARD GUILPIN
*SKIALETHIA* · 1598

or stacks of freshly baked Stratford loaves, still warm enough to make the nostrils twitch. In the tumbledown riverside taverns of Ratcliffe and Wapping drunken sailors are still snoring, the potboys are emptying their slops back into barrels to sell again to the day's first customers and the local drabs are quietly taking their leave down the back alleys with whatever they have been paid or taken.

On the streets of London itself blue-smocked apprentices are taking down the shutters of their masters' workshops. The Statute of Artificers decrees that between mid-March and mid-September everyone must be at work by 5 o'clock in the morning and

*Street life. London's thoroughfares are thronged with vendors crying their wares.*

[33]

Rustica Anglicana.    Modus vendendi Lupos pisces apud Anglos.

continue until 7 o'clock in the evening, though two-and-a-half hours may be taken between those times for meals and breaks. Between mid-September and mid-March work is to begin at first light and continue until dusk.

In strict Puritan households, which are numerous in some city parishes, families gather for prayer and a reading from the Scriptures before setting about the business of the day, conscious of doing the Lord's work and knowing that this day, as every day, may be the day of their death and a reckoning of their mortal deeds.

At the city's inns there is clatter and chatter in the courtyards, as ostlers harness horses ready for their departing owners and maids hover hopefully for a tip. Schoolboys hurry – or dawdle – on their way to the classroom, the more conscientious murmuring the conjugation of a half-remembered Latin irregular verb, the rowdy sidling up to their fellows to snatch a woollen cap and throw it into a heap of horse-

*Country higglers bearing their home produce.*

droppings. All around them stallholders pile their produce to best advantage, covering stale items with fresh and crying their wares to passersby – 'Cherry ripe, apples fine!' 'What do ye lack? – Pins, points, garters or ribbons of silk?'

Between 7 and 8 o'clock working people snatch a hasty breakfast. As this is London, the greatest city in the kingdom, the bread will be white, the beer will be good and there will be butter as well as cheese or a herring. Some of the country market people will already be heading for home. The lucky ones will have sold up all they have brought, the shrewd ones will know that it is a better use of time to get rid of unsold produce to a stallholder and get back to work than hang about the rest of the day trying to unload it.

By mid-morning the Royal Exchange (p. 93), the focal point of the city's commercial life, is buzzing with richly gowned men of business doing deals in a dozen tongues, while the dazzling Court at Whitehall (p. 95) is all rumours and whispers in the language of flattery and deceit as ministers and maids of honour ready themselves to enter the royal presence. Merchants in their counting-houses make piles of shillings, florins and ducats. Others crowd the riverside wharves to eye the cargoes unloading from ships that have just arrived in port, or seek out their masters to treat them in a tavern.

In their comfortable, if crowded, houses, the merchants' wives supervise the daily cleaning routine, dispatch servants to the streetmarkets for meat or fish, check that yesterday's washing has been properly aired and dried and plan more satisfying tasks, such as distilling, pickling and preserving. No sooner are these matters set in place than they must organize the preparations for the

*Housewives spread their laundry out to dry and air beyond the city walls.*

main meal of the day – trenchers to be scoured, spoons and knives laid out, the meal itself to be cooked and sauced and all to be ready half an hour before noon.

Elsewhere, in the homes of the truly wealthy, the pace is more leisurely. The organization of meals and household chores is delegated to male servants, who chivvy the female ones. The mistress of the house, even if not particularly devout, has time to read a devotional book, to which she can refer knowingly to her pew-neighbours in church on Sunday. Alternatively she may venture forth to Cheapside (p. 100) to purchase gloves or a ruff or napery or a gift for a christening. Her daughters, meanwhile, take private lessons in French and music and unpick the faults in yesterday's embroidery.

In the Marshalsea prison in Southwark a well-practised cozener puts his enforced idleness to fruitful use by fashioning loaded dice.

Between 11 and 2 o'clock the streets are at their busiest, with people hurrying to and from their homes to eat the main meal of the day, while those too far from home crowd the taverns and ordinaries. Anticipation of a good meal and fear of being late make people inattentive to all but their immediate purpose. It is a time of day much favoured by pickpockets.

By 2 o'clock everyone who should be back at work is so. In the eating-houses the potboys and serving wenches gather up the broken bread and scrape

*Model family. A wife and children listen closely to the head of the household, as they should.*

up the leftovers so that they can be added into a great cauldron of pottage permanently simmering in the back kitchen. Over on the south side of the city the gallants of the court, the gentlemen students of the Inns of Court and visitors to the city in search of its most famous entertainments, mix with honest citizens who have deemed it prudent to treat their wives to an afternoon out – and all foregather, according to the day, to enjoy the pleasures of the playhouse, or the thrill of seeing a bear or a bull tormented by snarling mastiffs (see p. 129). Ferrying the playgoers across the river has kept scores of watermen at their busiest for the last two hours and now many snooze at their oars, recovering their strength.

With the midday meal cleared away but the house still empty of schoolboys and husbands, the housewife takes advantage of an interval of calm to potter in her garden, repair clothing or even gossip with a neighbour. In her stillroom she may make soap, scented with roses or lavender, or concoct a batch of mouthwash – two parts honey, two parts vinegar and one part white wine.

At 5 o'clock the school day ends and the streets are once again boisterous with shrill voices and mischief at the expense of crippled beggars or tired stallholders packing away their unsold wares. By the time that darkness falls the evening meal is being consumed. Strict regulations forbid skilled craftsmen, such as tailors, to work by artificial light in case they fall short of the highest standards and thus imperil the reputation of their craft. In theory householders should hang a light out in front of their houses; many fail to do so.

Most families say their prayers together, check the doors and windows, damp down the fire and turn in. In the streets around, in the alehouses, taverns and inns, the noise of eating, drinking, dancing, singing, swearing and occasionally brawling, will continue for hours by the smoky light of smelly tallow candles. In the homes of the wealthy, expensive wax candles burn with a light bright enough to enable the master to sit up late to read or write letters without distraction. Outside, on the mud-spattered streets of the splendid, squalid city the voice of the watchman calls into the darkness:

*Give ear to the clock,*
*Beware your lock,*
*Your fire and your light,*
*And God give you goodnight,*
*Ten o'clock!*

### LONDONERS BORN

Most Londoners were born in the city and are immensely proud of the fact. But though Londoners may be slow to acknowledge it, the city is not the healthiest of places. Every year more die than are born and at least 5,000 newcomers are needed annually just to make up the shortfall. For the city to increase in numbers, thousands more must arrive. And, except in years of plague, they do. The largest numbers are young men seeking an apprenticeship or work, and young women seeking a position in service and, perhaps, a husband. They come mainly from the surrounding counties of Middlesex, Surrey, Kent, Essex and Hertfordshire. Others come from every

## LONDON LANGUAGE

*abroad* – out of doors
*alien, stranger* – a resident foreigner
*artificer* – skilled workman
*blue-coat* – a servant
*cozener* – confidence trickster
*firing* – firewood
*higgler* – pedlar
*jakes* – a privy
*jetty* – upper floor, protruding forward over the front of a house
*journeyman* – worker who has completed his apprenticeship but is employed (originally by the day [*jour*]) and not yet an independent master
*napery* – table linen
*ordinary* – eating-house, also the fixed-price, set meal it serves
*paled* – fenced
*potboy* – youth employed to clear away in a tavern
*pottage* – dense soup or stew, usually thickened with stale bread and flavoured with scraps of meat and vegetables
*watchman* – parish officer appointed to patrol streets by night

part of the realm and neighbouring lands, so that on the streets or in the alehouses you may hear every accent of England, not to mention the outlandish tongues – Scottish, Irish, Welsh, Cornish and Manx. And then there are the foreigners.

## LONDONERS MADE

London has substantial resident populations from beyond the seas. These are concentrated in the parish of St Olave's, Southwark, at the southern end of London Bridge, around Blackfriars and in St Martin's-le-Grand. A 'Return of Strangers', undertaken for the Bishop of London in 1593, reckoned their numbers at 7,000, almost exactly the same as a similar survey undertaken 20 years ago. Over a third of the present alien population has been born in England.

The most noticeable of the foreigners are those out of Africa, obvious not in numbers but in terms of their appearance, by virtue of their complexion, hair and features. The English distinguish between 'Moors', who come from Morocco and North Africa, 'Ethiops' who are out of the interior of Africa, and 'Blackamoors' who are from the western coasts of Africa. Most have arrived in England through no wish of their own – unless they have escaped from somewhere worse. They are not sufficient in numbers to have even one church or school of their own. But at least they are not slaves, for no one can be held a slave in England.

The largest single group of alien residents are what the English call 'the Doche', in which group they lump together the Dutch, the Flemish and the Germans. They have their own church at the former Augustinian monastery, now known as Austin Friars. In Southwark the Flemish in particular are renowned as brewers and prostitutes. London's Dutch do business and intermarry with other Dutch communities in Colchester and Norwich.

The other major community are the French Protestants, known as Huguenots, who first arrived in 1550 and have the church of St Anthony in Three Needle Street. There are other Huguenot communities at Canterbury, Sandwich and as far away as Exeter.

Members of both the French and Dutch communities continue to speak their own native languages, as well as English, to marry among themselves and to take on each other's children as apprentices, but they also play their part in community affairs and do not limit their charity work to their own kind.

Most aliens have the status of 'denizen', which gives them the right to carry out a trade and to have the protection of the law for their lives and property, but not to hold office as, for

*Pigs and Frenchmen speak one language: awee, awee!*

WILLIAM HAUGHTON
ENGLISHMEN FOR
MY MONEY • 1598

instance, an alderman or magistrate. Aliens are also bound to pay extra taxes, obliged to employ as many English as foreign in their businesses and are required to make their wills in Latin so that they may be clearly understood. Londoners' attitudes to aliens are contradictory. That 'strangers' chose England as their refuge makes the English proud as champions of liberty and conscience. But, inevitably, the incomers are blamed for many of the city's ills. They are accused of splitting decent family homes to create squalid, overcrowded tenements, of taking in illegal lodgers who ought to be whipped out of London as vagabonds, of undercutting wage rates, of sending their profits abroad. In Parliament Sir Walter Ralegh (p. 77) has complained that it is simply unfair to Englishmen that the Dutch work so hard. Many suspect that they come not for freedom of worship, but for freedom to prosper at English expense.

Anyone who cares for London's prosperity, however, will know that foreigners have made a contribution out of all proportion to their numbers. Thanks to Huguenot weavers London bids fair to have its own manufacture of silks and velvets. The production of green glassware was established by an Italian, Verzelini. The art of starching was introduced by a Dutch matron, Dingen Van der Passe. In the same year, 1564, another Dutch newcomer, Guylliam Bonen, introduced the first coach to the streets of London and since then a whole new craft of coachbuilding has been developed. A German, Peter Moritz, was the first to harness the tidal flow of the Thames to supply water to houses. London's aliens are shoemakers, schoolteachers, sculptors, silversmiths and surgeons, clockmakers and printers, diamond-cutters, featherdressers and perfumers of gloves, makers of buttons, tennis racquets, crossbows and playing-cards, masons,

## LONDON LIVING

Huguenot habits are catching on with other Londoners. Because weavers have to spend all day at their looms they brighten their workrooms by growing fragrant flowers in wooden boxes which they hang at the windows and keep caged canaries by them for the sweetness of their singing.

Thrifty Huguenot housewives have shown their neighbours that the tail of an ox should not be thrown away as useless but can be braised to make a hearty stew and the bones and leftovers rendered into a delicious soup.

They also gather scraps of meat to make a spicy, scarlet sausage called a saveloy. This can be eaten hot or cold and has become a great favourite with those whose work compels them to eat on the streets or on the move, such as porters and carriers. It is said that the main ingredient that gives the saveloy its distinctive flavour and texture is brains, but this may be only a rumour.

apothecaries and cartographers. Without their mastery of their mysteries this city would be so much less than it is – and will be.

## LONDONERS PROPER

IF, AS A VISITOR, YOU CAN'T GET AWAY from that feeling of being an outsider, derive some comfort from the fact that about a quarter of London's adult male residents are, in a real sense, outsiders too.

No man can be reckoned a full citizen of London unless he is a member of a City Company, because only these are allowed to own property, employ others, and vote for the Lord Mayor, Sheriffs, Aldermen etc. Unskilled workers, about one man in every four, are therefore excluded from its affairs. In many cities these Companies would be known as craft or merchant guilds, depending on whether they were mainly concerned with making and selling goods or simply dealing in them. In London they are more usually known as Livery Companies because their most senior members are entitled to wear an elaborate uniform or livery, usually lined with silk or velvet and

*This also hath been common in England, contrary to the customs of all other nations, and yet to be seen (for example, in most streets of London) that many of our greatest houses have outwardly been very simple and plain to sight, which inwardly have been able to receive a duke with his whole train and lodge them at their ease ... moreover ... the fronts of our streets have not been so uniform and orderly builded as those of foreign cities.*

WILLIAM HARRISON
*DESCRIPTION OF ENGLAND*

trimmed with fur. These are worn when members of a company feast in its hall or when they are conducting official business.

The authority of the Livery Companies is not to be ignored, since infractions are punishable by a fine or confiscation of faulty goods, and apprentices may be whipped. Recalcitrant or persistent offenders may be expelled from the company. Wily newcomers, especially foreigners, tend to settle in areas like Southwark, where they can ply a trade free from official control because the authority of the companies does not normally extend further than the boundaries of the City.

The city is totally dominated by members of the 'Great Twelve' livery companies:

The Mercers come first. Dealing in the most expensive imported textiles such as silks, satins and velvets, they have many customers at Court and often serve as money-lenders to their well-connected – and extravagant – customers as well.

The second most important company is the Grocers, followed by the Drapers, Fishmongers, Goldsmiths, Skinners, Merchant Taylors, Haberdashers, Salters,

Ironmongers, Vintners and Cloth-workers.

There are separate companies for distinct branches of the same business, as in the case of makers of wax and tallow candles.

Sometimes they will merge together as the Blacksmiths have with the Spurriers, the Leathersellers with the Pouchmakers and the Bakers of white bread with the Bakers of brown bread.

If you are yourself involved in commerce or a craft, seek out a Londoner in your line of work. Don't expect too much in the way of sharing professional secrets – a craft isn't known as a 'mystery' for nothing – but time your approach when one of their feasts is in the offing and you might just find yourself invited to what will almost certainly be a memorable meal.

## FIRST CITIZEN

WITHIN THE CITY OF LONDON ONLY the sovereign herself outranks the Lord Mayor, chosen annually from the Masters of one of the 12 Great Companies. He must first have served as an Alderman and as a Sheriff. The term of office lasts a single year but it is possible, though not usual, to serve more than once. As he is expected to keep open house only a rich man can contemplate serving in this office. Any foreign visitor of the slightest distinction, for example, will be invited to dine at the house of the Lord Mayor.

The Lord Mayor is responsible for maintaining good order, dispensing justice, organizing emergency food supplies when famine threatens,

*Make Way! The unmistakable figure of the Lord Mayor, preceded by his sword-bearer.*

[41]

enforcing health regulations in time of plague, keeping a count of foreigners and supervising the operation of the city's many markets.

You can scarcely fail to catch a glimpse of the Lord Mayor as he goes about in public, recognizable by his great gold chain of office and his splendid fur-trimmed scarlet robe; in front of him strides his official sword-bearer, wearing a fur cap and holding a great sword pointing upwards – not to serve as his bodyguard but in token of the Lord Mayor's authority. When a former Lord Mayor dies he usually leaves generous legacies for the relief of the poor, the building of almshouses, the repair of churches and other such causes.

In the conduct of his official business the Lord Mayor relies heavily on the Aldermen, there being one for each of the 26 wards into which the city is divided. Through his deputies the Alderman of each ward sees to the appointment and performance of constables, watchmen, scavengers and other minor officers. So great is the authority of the Alderman within his ward that anyone who dares to strike him would be condemned to lose the offending arm.

## HOMES

THANKS TO DECADES OF PEACE English houses are no longer made for defence but for comfort. The newly rich may still build turrets, battlements and gatehouses but these are only for show or to make a new place look venerable, implying an ancient lineage for themselves. Many a country house still has a moat, though the fact that it seldom runs right around it should tell you that it is not to keep attackers at bay – or for you to water your horse in – but to keep fish for the kitchen.

Travelling towards London the visitor will note many of the better dwellings called 'Abbey' or 'Priory', being a former monastery made over into the residence of a gentleman. In London itself a few great houses are

built of stone, if ancient or made of the fabric of some religious house now dissolved. But these are exceptional, there being no building stone within 40 miles of the city.

Londoners favour houses built of frames of timber, filled in either with laths and daub of earth, dung and straw or with brick, locally baked, according to the wealth of the householder. The usual height runs to three storeys, though some are of four or even five, with upper floors thrusting further forward than the lower by 2 or 3 ft. This feature, a jetty, wins the householder more space in upper rooms, though at the expense of darkening the street outside. Oak, the most widely used building timber, is honoured particularly by the English as a symbol of their nation, being the strongest wood. During the reign of the present Queen the main changes in the homes of Londoners have been the building of staircases, instead of ladders, to reach upper rooms, the making of brick fireplaces and chimneys and the creation of indoor privies.

In London the home of almost every citizen has casements of glass, some showing their coat of arms in colours. Only the poorest dwellings, and low alehouses, still have windows of lattice, covered with oiled cloth or parchment. In the better houses rainwater from the roof collects in lead-lined tanks, being both softer for washing and less suspect in crowded London than water drawn from a well.

The chambers of the wealthiest citizens' houses have wooden panelling, called wainscot, and are often painted in red, white and green, the colours of Her Majesty. A few follow the Spanish fashion for moulded leather panelling, coloured gold and black, particularly useful where food may be cooked or

*The walls of our houses on the inner sides ... be either hanged with tapestry, arras work or painted cloths, wherein divers histories, or herbs, beasts, knots and such like are stained ... whereby the rooms are not a little commended, made warm and much more close than otherwise they would be.*

WILLIAM HARRISON
*DESCRIPTION OF ENGLAND*

## LONDON LIVING

Where there is space, new houses are often laid out in the plan of the letter E to admit more light and as a compliment to the name of Elizabeth, the Queen, as once they were built as H for Harry, her father. Puritans, being by nature contrary, maintain that if they build a house on this plan the E stands for Emanuel, Our Lord in Heaven. As a great port London has many shipbuilders and when an old ship comes to the end of its useful life its larger timbers, hardened by exposure to the elements, may be sold on to be built into houses.

served because, unlike textiles, it does not retain smells. The richest have tapestries. In most homes, however, the walls of the rooms seen by outsiders are decorated either with paintings actually on the plaster of the walls or with hanging cloths showing scenes from the Bible or the history and myths of the Greeks and Romans. The much favoured parable of the Prodigal Son features scenes of open hospitality, recalling to Londoners the wealth of their city; its depictions of poverty serve as a sobering reminder of the calloused beggar at the end of every street. Londoners also like the tale of Susannah and the Elders – nudity shown without fear of censure, the story being from the Old Testament.

Floors are usually covered with mats of woven or plaited rushes. You will find these springy to walk on and, when new, give off a pleasant, fresh smell. You'll know you are in a very wealthy home when you see Turkey carpets being used to cover tables, beds and chests. Chests have multiple uses – to store linen, bedding, books, clothes etc. and to serve as extra seating or, in bedrooms, as stands for a looking-glass or a basin and ewer.

Be grateful if you have someone to make up your bed for you because it's a real chore. The English loathe draughts and believe good sleep essential for healthy living. As a result their best beds are like miniature fortresses against the cold, with a rope frame, on top of which is a canvas sheet, a straw pallet, a feather mattress, good linen sheets, warm woollen blankets and finally a counterpane. A tester above and curtains around the bed complete the nocturnal defences. Some Londoners think it more vital to wear a nightcap even than a nightgown. Almost all wear a night kerchief to keep their throat warm.

Household guests will find themselves provided with towels, soap – usually home-made and all the better for it – and, to clean their teeth, a tooth soap and a strip of rough linen cloth.

## LONDON LIVING

While it is both perfectly legal and socially acceptable to discipline servants with a beating that inflicts pain but not lasting injury, many householders find it more effective to employ a system of fines. The following scale is fairly usual:

If a cook fails to produce a meal on time – half a day's wages.

Attempting improper relations with a maid – 4 pence.

Teaching the children of the house bawdy words – 4 pence.

Absence from a meal or prayers – 2 pence.

An oath – one penny for each occasion. Ditto leaving open a door that was found shut.

For leaving a bed unmade or a fireplace unswept after 8 o'clock – one penny.

For a dirty shirt or a missing button on Sunday – 6 pence.

Any male servant striking another or provoking another to strike to be subject to instant dismissal.

The notion of upholstered furniture is scarcely known outside the court, apart from plentiful cushions. Children and servants sit on benches and stools but in many homes the master now sits in a chair with arms.

In a well-run house a good wife will change the linen tablecloths and napkins twice a week. In the best houses a cupboard stands in the dining-room to show off the family's collection of silver. Bowls, platters and tankards may bear an engraved coat of arms, evidence of gentle status newly acquired. The owner doubtless experiences a quiet glow of pride every time he glances at it. His wife knows that engraved plate simply gathers grime more quickly and needs polishing more often.

> *God Almighty first planted a garden. And indeed it is the purest of human pleasures. It is the greatest refreshment to the spirits of man; without which buildings and palaces are but gross handiworks.*
> FRANCIS BACON • OF GARDENS

## GARDENS

I F YOU ARE INVITED TO STAY IN A Londoner's house and want to make a good first impression, you simply cannot do better than to ask for a tour of the garden. Gardens are a passion with the English and Londoners are no exception to this rule. The Queen herself is said to work in her palace gardens every morning, seriously and briskly, with her own hands, pruning and even weeding, not just supervising.

There is an eager readership for books about gardening. The most well known, by Thomas Hill, first appeared as a *Most Brief and Pleasant Treatise teaching how to Dress, Sow and Set a Garden.* The author has successfully prolonged

*Neither chore nor bore – Londoners actually enjoy gardening.*

its life by calling the second edition *The Profitable Art of Gardening* and including a new section on bee-keeping. The third version, published under the name of Didymus Mountain (not Hill!) was called *The Gardener's Labyrinth*, with an extra section on grafting. Three more editions have since appeared but the author has moved on to writing about the science of physiognomy, the interpretation of dreams, the meaning of comets and how to master arithmetic.

When being shown round a garden which is clearly meant to impress, you should look out for and make a suitably complimentary comment about:
(a) Patterned parterres defined by close-clipped hedges of box.

(b) Paths of different coloured earths, gravels and sand. These are troublesome to keep immaculate but many householders will bear the expense for the sake of the effect.
(c) Fountains – much favoured as better than still pools, which attract tiresome flies and frogs.
(d) Arbours that are made of ash, which lasts ten years, rather than of willow, which decays in three, so ash is the choice of those who are better-off.
(e) Brick walls store up and reflect back the heat from the sun, making it possible to grow foreign exotics, such as apricots or peaches, against them.

*The very latest thing for the garden, a powerful pump to give parterres that dew-fresh look.*

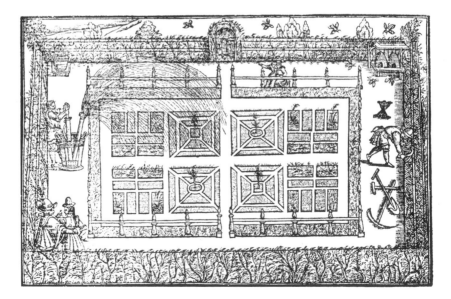

The largest gardens have space for a bowling green and an artificial mount, with tables and benches or even a banqueting house, from which the host and his guests can look down on his garden – and over his neighbours' walls.

More usually the town garden serves more mundane purposes – to grow herbs for cooking, cosmetics and medicines, to raise fresh lettuce, peas and beans for the table, to grow plums or cherries and to keep bees. For the hardpressed housewife not the least advantage of a good-sized garden is having somewhere safe and convenient to dry the washing. Those without one have to carry a heavy basket of wet washing out to Finsbury Fields or Mile End Waste to spread it out on hedges and bushes. Apart from the time and trouble taken in doing this there is always the risk of theft. Stealing items left out to dry is probably London's most common crime.

*If you look into our gardens … how wonderfully is their beauty increased, not only with flowers … but also with rare and medicinable herbs sought up in the land within these forty years; so that, in comparison of this present, the ancient gardens were but dunghill … It is a world also to see how many strange herbs, plants and annual*

> **LONDON LORE**
> The rose is the national flower of England and the badge of the Queen herself.
> Rosewater is essential for washing, cooking, perfumes and many medicines.
> The Temple is famous for its roses, where the quarrel that began the Wars of the Roses is held to have been the House of York snatching a white rose for its badge, the House of Lancaster a red.

*fruits are daily brought unto us from the Indies.*

WILLIAM HARRISON
*DESCRIPTION OF ENGLAND*

*Chambers and parlours strawed over with sweet herbs, refreshed me, their nosegays finely intermingled with sundry sorts of flowers in their bedchambers and privy rooms, with comfortable smell cheered me up and entirely delighted all my senses.*

LEVIE LEMNIE,
DUTCH PHYSICIAN
*THE TOUCHSTONE OF COMPLEXIONS* • 1576

Londoners in particular benefit from ever-growing trading links that the city has with distant countries with different climates and crops. Seeds are easily brought back and sometimes living plants are successfully transported to be nurtured by skilled gardeners and so adapted to the English soils and air. The wealthiest Londoners can now enjoy homegrown exotics such as peaches, apricots, melons, lemons, oranges and pomegranates, while even ordinary gardens are brightened by the nasturtium and the larkspur. Sometimes the names of these newcomers are somewhat misleading. The 'African marigold' actually comes from Mexico, as does the 'Spanish bayonet' or yucca plant.

Apart from the grounds of the royal palaces the most impressive gardens are those of the Inns of Court and the City Companies. The Walks at Gray's Inn are lined with ancient elms and brilliant with woodbines, eglantines, pinks, violets and vines. Lincoln's Inn has grass lawns of a rich emerald green and a warren for rabbits for the table. The garden of the Drapers' Company is renowned for damask roses and has a maze, a fountain and a bowling alley. The Goldsmiths are so wealthy that they have two gardens, one next to their hall on Cheapside and another, with a banqueting house, beyond Cripplegate.

Perhaps the most remarkable garden of any individual is that of Hugh Platt, the gentleman resident at Kirby's Castle, Bethnal Green. Here he has conducted many experiments with different kinds of manure and grown a vineyard whose wine has been complimented by the French ambassador, who said truly they had none like it in France. Platt has compiled a handbook of hints for housewives covering such diverse skills as distilling cordials, preserving fruits and dyeing hair under the heading of *Delights for Ladies to Adorn their Persons, Tables, Closets and Distillatories with Beauties, Banquets, Perfumes and Waters.*

Londoners who do not have the amenity of a garden at the back of their dwelling often rent a garden outside the city walls to use in much the same way as their more fortunate neighbours – to grow herbs, fruit and salad plants, to take the air with family or friends of an evening or on holidays, and to play games. Though there are those whose purposes are, perhaps, less innocent …

*In the fields and suburbs … they have their gardens either paled (fenced) or walled about very high … and lest they might be espied in these open places they have their Banqueting houses … wherein they may, and doubtless do, many of them play the filthy persons … their gardens are locked … where they, meeting their sweethearts, receive their wished desires.*

PHILIP STUBBES • *THE ANATOMY OF ABUSES*

SINE SOLE
RIS.

I *This 'Rainbow Portrait' can be seen at Hatfield House, home of the Cecils, the Queen's closest councillors.* Non Sine Sole Iris – *No Rainbow without Sun – refers to the rain, a symbol of peace after strife, which the Queen holds in her right hand.*
II (Following pages) *The Queen en route to a society wedding in the fashionable residential district of Blackfriars. Although the Queen looks as though she is being carried in a litter she is in fact riding on a concealed chariot, pushed by the Yeomen of the Guard (in red) at the rear.*

III (Above) *Four gentlemen playing Primero, a favourite game of Her Majesty. As in Spain, France and Italy a pack of 40 cards is used, the 8s, 9s and 10s being removed and each card given a points value different from its face value. This being England, after that the rules are somewhat different ...*

IV (Left) *Robert Devereux, second Earl of Essex, painted in 1596, the year in which he became a national hero by raiding the Spanish naval base at Cadiz.*

V (Right) *Sir Walter Ralegh, with his eldest son, also Walter. After a period of banishment from Court Ralegh is once more in favour with Her Majesty.*

VI (Below) *Dessert at the home of Lord Cobham and his family – fruit and nuts are served on silver plates and the pet parrot leaves its table-top perch to join in.*
VII (Opposite) *John Banister lecturing on anatomy to the members of the Company of Barber-Surgeons. He and his four colleagues all wear white protective over-sleeves. Attendance at these sessions is compulsory for members of the company. The approved textbook shown here is* De Re Anatomica, *published in Paris in 1562 by Realdo Colombo, pupil and successor to the great Vesalius.*
VIII (Opposite below) *A Maundy Medallion. One of nine miniatures painted to illustrate the work of the Sovereign. The Flemish artist, Levina Teerlinc, pioneered the art of the miniature painting in England and became a Gentlewoman of the Queen's household.*

IX *Home comforts. The home of courtier and diplomat Sir Henry Unton at Wadley in Berkshire. Sir Henry is shown in scholarly solitude at the top of the house in a library lined with over 200 books. To the left below he and his friends play viols. The main picture shows a banquet scene where the diners, having finished their meal, are being entertained with a masque to musical accompaniment.*

# IV· THE INNER MAN
# – AND WOMAN

*New Foods, New Foibles · Manners & Mealtimes*
*Banquets · Tobacco*

*The situation of our region, lying near unto the north, doth cause the heat of our stomachs to be of somewhat greater force; therefore our bodies do crave a little more ample nourishment than the inhabitants of the hotter regions.*

WILLIAM HARRISON
*DESCRIPTION OF ENGLAND*

Londoners eat heartily. Only Puritans fast – and Turks. So unless you are either a Puritan or a Turk, don't think people will admire you for fasting.

> *It is almost impossible to believe that they could eat so much meat in one city alone.*
>
> ALESSANDRO MAGNO
> OF VENICE • 1562

---

### MEAT

---

Meat, especially beef, comes top of the Londoner's list of favourite foods. Because the surrounding countryside cannot meet the demand for it, cattle are driven to London from as far away as Wales. The long journey makes them lean and stringy, so you can usually see them grazing on the marshes to the east of the city to fatten them up again.

If the poor can afford meat it is normally bacon. The English are the only people in Europe known for eating collops with eggs. Horse-meat is never (knowingly) eaten but might well be mixed in with other fillings in pies or sausages. London butchers' shops, stalls and slaughterhouses are under constant inspection, so this is not likely to happen within the city walls. What comes in from the countryside is another matter. Country folk still eat badgers and hedgehogs. So think twice about buying pasties sold on the streets from a basket rather than from a regular (and regulated) baker's shop.

Occasionally a worn out work-ox will be bought for distribution among the poor. Before it can be made edible it will either be beaten, pounded, fried, diced or stewed for hours until its meat can be added to a pottage for flavouring.

*Weather permitting, Londoners like to eat outdoors in the summer.*

**Poultry** The swan is the most expensive dish that can be bought in the regular markets and is normally only eaten at feasts. Most water-birds, like mallards or herons, are served with a sauce made from their own blood, made piquant with spices and thickened with breadcrumbs. Goose is usually eaten roasted, with sorrel sauce or mustard and vinegar. The tastiest poultry are ducklings from Aylesbury and turkeys from Norfolk. Pigeons are cheap at 8 pence a dozen and make a common pie filling.

**Game** Hare and coney are common and cheap. In theory deer, raised in the parks of the aristocracy and protected by law, can neither be bought nor sold. A fine buck, therefore, is often presented as a gift but the beast does somehow find its way onto the market, if not the open market. Deer certainly features regularly in the feasts of the Livery Companies of London.

If not stewed or made into a pie, both meat and fish are usually cooked with a stuffing. This might typically include figs, raisins, sugar, pork fat, breadcrumbs and egg yolks and any of a hundred combinations of herbs and spices.

*Venison is a lord's dish, good for an Englishman, for it doth animate him to be as he is, which is strong and hardy; beef is a good meat for an English man, so be it the beast be young, and that it be not cow-flesh … veal is good and easily digested; bacon is for carters and ploughmen, the which be ever labouring.*

DR ANDREW BOORDE
*A BREVIARY OF HEALTH* • 1542

### DIET

From a health point of view the diet of the rich is poor. They eat so much meat that they suffer from not eating enough vegetables, fruit or milk products. Early in adult life they are liable to contract a touch of scurvy and suffer from loose teeth; later there will come bladder problems, kidney pains and failing eyesight.

### EATING FOR ENGLAND

Fish is patriotic. England broke with Rome long ago but the English are still supposed to eat fish on Fridays, and Wednesdays and Saturdays as well. This is intended, in the words regularly read from the pulpit, 'for the increase of fishermen, of whom do spring mariners to go upon the sea, to the furnishing of the Navy of the Realm'. Catch cod today, sink Spaniards tomorrow.

The ban on meat-eating should apply 156 days a year, but is strictly enforced only in Lent. Breaking the Lenten ban means a hefty fine or six hours in the pillory, or a night in the stocks or ten days in a lock-up. In fact, 'meatless' days are not so hard to put up with because poultry, puffins, veal and game

## LONDON LANGUAGE

*amulet* – omelette
*Barbary* – North Africa
*Carbonado* – to slash with a knife for grilling
*collops* – fried rashers of bacon
*cullis* – meat broth
*drage* – rye + barley
*green goose* – goose under four months old
*guinea fowl* – resembles a partridge, new from West Africa
*kickshaw* – fancy snack, from French *quelquechose* = something
*Levant* – eastern coast of the Mediterranean
*marchpane* – marzipan
*maslin* – rye + wheat
*nunchion* – snack between meals
*poor John* – salted hake
*pottle* – tankard containing two quarts
*rabbit* – a coney under one year old
*rear-banquet* – late night snack
*sack* – sherry
*seeth* – simmer
*stockfish* – air-dried cod, usually from Norway
*stubble goose* – goose fattened by gleaning fields after harvest
*sucket* – sweet e.g. sugar-plum
*verjuice* – sour juice of crab apples, from French *vert jus* = green juice
*whiskey* – a strong distilled spirit, from the Irish *ulsce beathadh* = water of life

accompanied by three dishes of fish. Invalids can buy an exemption licence from their bishop. The money goes to the poor-box, not the bishop. A licensed meat-eater always makes a useful dinner guest. A meat dish may be set before him – which he may wish to share round.

Salted fish is a winter staple and should be cooked and seasoned accordingly. Stockfish can be kept for years at a time and is therefore an essential item in naval and garrison stores. But it literally needs breaking down to be made edible, so most cooks will have their own 'stockfish hammer' for doing this. The best books recommend beating for an hour, then soaking it overnight, then boiling it for at least two hours before attempting to turn it into a soup, stew or pie.

Oysters are eaten in vast quantities – from the shell, in pies and patties or as a thickening for soups, stews and stuffings. The best oysters come from Colchester in Essex and Whitstable in Kent. The best trout comes from Hampshire. Salmon pickled in brine is brought from Scotland. Like conger eel it is usually poached in a strong ale. Pike is regarded as the king of fish. Carp are rare and much prized. The poor eat eels and shellfish.

### CHOOSE CHEESE

On meatless days many choose cheese. English soldiers get half a pound a day as their regular rations. Go to

all count as 'fish'. Eggs, however, are forbidden in Lent, even as an ingredient.

On Wednesdays it is permitted to serve one dish of meat providing it is

## LONDON LIVING

Sugar is another common craving of the wealthy. The Queen is addicted to sugared almonds – whence the discoloration and gaps in her teeth. (NB English portraits never show people grinning.) Sugar loaves can be bought in Fish Street. English honey – far less damaging to the teeth – is excellent and exported throughout Europe.

Leadenhall Market or Bread Street for premium English cheeses like tangy Cheddar or crumbly Cheshire. For Londoners the most common kind is made in Essex and Suffolk from ewes' milk. It tastes sharp and comes in huge, rock-hard blocks you could use to patch a castle wall. This kind is standard fare for sailors – not that they like it:

*Those that made me were uncivil,*
*They made me harder than the devil.*
*Knives can't cut me, fire won't light me,*
*Dogs bark at me but can't bite me.*

### GETTING YOUR GREENS

Nobody actually likes vegetables that much, except for onions from Flanders and cabbages, which are often chopped up in soups. Otherwise vegetables are tolerated, especially when served swimming in butter. The best butter comes from Epping in Essex. Inferior varieties may be coloured with the juice squeezed from marigold leaves and then passed off in the market as Epping butter.

Vegetables are often boiled with grain into a sludge called pottage – common in the countryside but only fit for the beggar's bowl in London. Beetroot, red cabbage, mushrooms, cucumbers and samphire are preserved in vinegar, verjuice or stale beer for winter eating.

Fruit is abundant but, for safety's sake, seldom eaten raw, but rather baked, boiled or pulped. Diet experts advise eating plums, damsons, cherries and grapes at the beginning of a meal 'to open the stomach', and dense fruits, like pears, apples or nuts at the end of the meal 'to close it'. English strawberries are small, sweet and superb and may be served in red wine with sugar, cinnamon and ginger. The strawberry season lasts only a few weeks from mid-June. Prices vary widely from a shilling a pint to 3 pence. Cherries may be served with cinnamon, ginger – and mustard. Oranges, raisins, prunes and apricots are imported from Portugal and Spain but

*All manner of fruit generally fill the blood with water, which boileth up in the body as new wine doth in the vessel and so prepareth and causeth the blood to putrefy and consequently bringeth in sickness.*
DR THOMAS COGAN • 1584

## CAPITAL CAUTIONS!

A 'sallet' is any vegetable dish, raw or cooked – including a salad, which might come with primroses, daisies or dandelions.

'Good King Henry' is not a loyal toast but a sort of spinach with a peppery punch to it.

'Humbles' (say 'umbles') are entrails, usually of a deer, baked with herbs, spices and suet to make a 'humble pie'. The contents will include not only the heart, liver and kidneys but also the lungs, guts and spleen.

Brawn is a sort of stiff, meat paste made from the head and foreparts of a pig. It is considered a great treat, usually reserved for Christmas.

'Gravey' is a thick sauce of ground almonds, broth, sugar and ginger and is used to dress rabbit, chicken, eels or oysters.

'Blancmange' is remarkable for the absence of any strong spices in its preparation. The ingredients are boiled rice, capon flesh finely shredded with a pin, almond milk and sugar. The surface is usually decorated with blanched almonds. On fish days it may be made into a main dish by the addition of dried haddock, perch or lobster.

Beware of English mustard. It is incredibly hot and, if you are not used to it, should be tried with caution. Londoners use it especially to override the flavour of dried, salted fish.

cost a small fortune – 6 pence for a single lemon. If any of these appear on your host's table you'll know he's out to impress.

Many meat dishes are cooked in the manner of Barbary or the Levant, with fruit, such as prunes, oranges and dates, and spices, like mace and nutmeg. A common recipe for herring pie also includes a large pear, dates, raisins, currants, cinnamon, wine, butter, sugar and salt. Such dishes are cooked in a 'coffin' of hard, plain pastry, to keep the flavours and juices in. When the dish is cooked through, the coffin is discarded and not eaten.

### STAFF OF LIFE

Bread is the main filler. The rich, indeed most citizen householders of London, eat bread made from pure white flour. This is the best sort, known as manchet, made into round, flat loaves of 6 ounces. 'Cheat', 'ravel' or 'Yeoman's bread' has some of the bran left in and is greyish-yellow and made into large loaves. The poorest eat 'Carter's bread'. This may be made from rye or from maslin or from drage and lies longer in the stomach. When the harvest fails London bakers are ordered to make their loaves from oats, lentils, peas and, worst of all, beans.

Bread is also extensively used in cooking as a thickening agent, in the form of breadcrumbs as a coating and as an ingredient in the making of stuffings and sausages.

*Something special. Parading outsize bride-cakes baked for a wedding feast.*

## NEW FOODS, NEW FOIBLES

As a hub of international trade London is particularly open to foreign influences. What were once luxuries for the royal court have fallen so much in price that they can now be found in the houses of the merchants – such as sugar, pepper, almonds, dates etc. Olives are now brought from Greece, capers from France and anchovies from Spain. New foreign foods now include cucumbers, raspberries, spinach, aubergines, figs, asparagus, mulberries, kidney beans,

*Take prunes and put Claret Wine to them and Sugar, as much as you think will make them pleasant, let all these seeth together till ye think the Liquor look like a sirop and that your Prunes be well swollen.*

THE TREASURIE OF COMMODIOUS CONCEITS AND HIDDEN SECRETS • 1573

cauliflowers, sweet potatoes, globe artichokes and the very different Jerusalem artichoke, known as the 'potato of Canada'.

From the New World the English have taken the tomato and, believing it to be an aphrodisiac, have dubbed it the 'love apple'. John Gerard, the nation's leading herbalist, thinks it ought to be confined to the garden as a purely ornamental plant on account of its 'rank and stinking savour'. Gerard doesn't think much of maize either – 'it nourisheth but little and is of hard and evil digestion, a more convenient food for swine than man'.

The English have at last worked out which part of the 'Virginia potato' is poisonous (the leaves) and which part edible (the tubers). But so far no one has come up with a convincingly straightforward and appetizing way of eating it.

The Reverend Harrison has deplored the craze in noble households for employing foreign chefs – 'for the most part musical-headed Frenchmen' – who have brought with them their fricassees, hashes, bisques, ragouts, macaroons, the amulet and dozens of kinds of 'kickshaws'.

## LONDON LIVING

People with an estate within a day or so of the capital conduct two-way traffic in provisions, receiving fresh produce and sending back what can best be bought in London, whether it be salted fish or saffron. William Darrell's estates provided him with trout, venison, rabbits and chickens, as well as pheasant and partridge – even though these were out of season, and a special shipment of a dozen pigeon pies.

Darrell's Dutch gardener, Cornelius, even managed to send up three quarts of strawberries in mid-May, a month earlier than the regular crop. In return Darrell sent him back £1 3s and 3d worth of 'gardening stuff'.

Because Darrell's retinue did not include a personal chef he had to pay a cook a shilling a meal for 'dressing', roasting, frying or boiling his meat or fish and supplying an appropriate sauce made with parsley, cloves or sorrel.

## MANNERS & MEALTIMES

THE ORDINARY LONDON HOUSEHOLDER eats three times a day. Breakfast, taken between 6 and 7 o'clock, normally consists of bread and butter and perhaps herring, cold meat or cheese, depending on the season, washed down with ale. The midday meal may be eaten at a tavern or bought at a cookshop and taken home and will include a hot dish – a roast, pie, soup or stew – with the usual bread and beer. The evening supper, eaten at 5 or 6 o'clock, will be of cold meats, cheese and so on, with bread and beer.

Gentlemen and merchants eat their main meals slightly earlier and later – a cooked dinner between 11 o'clock and noon and a cooked supper at about 6 o'clock in the evening.

A family meal usually consists of two or three dishes, served simultaneously. If guests are present there may be four to six dishes and appetizers of salted radishes, salt beef with mustard or oysters with brown bread. Working people eat later, dining at noon and supping at 7 or 8 o'clock in the evening.

## BANQUETS

A BANQUET INVOLVES NOT ONLY A profusion of dishes but generally requires a centrepiece. A boar is a popular choice, but since it has been hunted to extinction, they must now be imported from France, so a boar's head, rather than a whole boar, is now more

## LONDON LIVING

The fork is known as an Italian affectation. But if you're fussy about these things do feel free to carry your own knife and spoon with you. Either way, make sure that you have washed your hands before you start eating – and that your fellow guests have seen you do so.

usual. The swan, heron, bustard, crane and peacock have fallen in favour but a young buck deer is still much prized. Wild birds from Surrey and Kent, like blackbirds, wheatears, dotterels and finches, are presented as appetizers. Samphire, gathered from the seashore, is another popular first dish.

Dishes will often be served by a professional carver, hired for the occasion. He will know how to deal with tricky items like a peacock or a porpoise, and which sauce should accompany which dish. So if you don't know the difference between trushing a chicken, splatting a pike and barbing a lobster leave it to the man who does.

It has become fashionable for the third and final course of a banquet to be taken in a separate room or, better still, a rustic arbour in a garden. In London houses it is common to go up onto the leads of the roof. There one consumes a picnic of sweets, tarts, jellies, fools, syllabubs, junkets, biscuits, comfits and preserves. Tart fillings may include pulped rosehips, petals of marigold,

cowslip or primrose beaten with cream or curds, or young peas flavoured with saffron, sugar, salt, verjuice and butter. Quinces are made into a stiff marmalade which may be moulded into fancy shapes and sprinkled with sugar.

### WATER

Water is for washing and cooking in. If it is to be used for diluting wine, take care first to strain then boil it. Best of all is to boil it into steam in an apparatus from which it can be recovered when distilled. Only then can you be really sure it's clean enough to drink without risk.

### ALE AND BEER

Ale is the regular household drink, usually brewed in three strengths – single, double and double-double. In 1560, soon after her accession, the Queen, who has strong opinions on the matter of beer, ordered that the brewing of double-double be stopped because it made people drunk so quickly, leading

*Mind your manners! Children may be expected to stand in the presence of adults, even at meal times.*

to brawls, stabbings etc. This decree was relatively easy to enforce in a closely regulated city like London, but outside its walls is quite another matter.

Ale may be flavoured with nutmeg, cinnamon or rosemary. Beer is ale with hops added to it. This imparts a bite to the flavour and enables the brew to be kept much longer. The terms ale and beer are frequently used as though they mean the same. A prosperous merchant household will brew its own beer once a month and produce about 200 gallons, which will usually be held over for a month before drinking. In noble households the beer will often be over a year old.

## LONDON LIVING

London's fishing port is Barking. When a Barking man goes off for a 16-week fishing season his daily victuals consist of a gallon of beer a day, a pound of hard-baked biscuit, 4 ounces of bacon, 3 ounces of oatmeal or dried peas, half a pound of Dutch cheese, a quarter of a pound of butter – and as much fresh fish as may be caught. There is also a daily ration of vinegar. In addition small quantities of flavourings are carried in the form of honey, sugar, pepper, nutmeg and ginger.

## MILK

As a general rule only the poor actually drink milk. However, milk, and even more importantly cream, are much used to make puddings, possets, junkets and trifles. If you do drink milk in London watch out for a distinctive back-taste. Many stall-kept cows are fed on brewers' waste mash. If you want it fresh from a well-kept cow this can be bought in St James's Park.

*I find … such heady ale and beer … as for the mightiness thereof among such as seek it out, is commonly called Huffcap, the Mad Dog, Father Whoreson and Dragons' Milk.*

WILLIAM HARRISON
A DESCRIPTION OF ENGLAND

## WINE

Most of England's vineyards were attached to religious houses so very few now survive, but the import trade from Gascony and the Rhineland stretches back over many centuries.

Wine is available in great variety. The most popular wines are claret, sack, malmsey and canary. Claret is usually 3 pence a pint, sack is 4 pence and Rhenish 5 pence. Wine is also imported from Spain, Portugal, Madeira and the islands of the Mediterranean, such as Corsica and Crete.

Wine is not sold in bottles and is therefore drunk from the wood. It is often diluted with water. The Queen herself takes three parts water to one part wine. Wines to be drunk cool are siphoned off from the barrel, then put into bottles to be chilled in a metal cistern of cold water. Wine is not normally kept past a year as it usually turns sour and vinegary.

For a true wine-lover therefore London is a paradise of choices. Unlike the Frenchman, who will praise the wines of his home region as the best, the Londoner has no domestic vintage to defend and so drinks as he wishes.

## AQUA VITAE

Alcohol distilled into a fiery spirit is newly popular, a taste spread by soldiers returning from the wars in the Netherlands and Ireland. Spiritous liquors give soldiers laughter in the tavern, warmth in the cold nights, courage in the fight and solace in defeat. Often called Aqua Vitae – Water of Life – these spirits are also and more accurately known as 'burning water'. They may be flavoured with juniper, wormwood, hyssop or mint. Such warming drinks are held to be good for the heart and are therefore known as 'cordials' and may be bought bottled from apothecaries.

*Smoking after a meal is thought to aid digestion.*

*The Irish Aquavitae, vulgarly called Usquebaugh [whiskey], is held the best in the world of that kind; which is made also in England, but nothing so good as that which is brought out of Ireland. And the Usquebaugh is preferred before our Aquavitae, because the mingling of raisins, fennel seed, and other things, mitigating the heat, and making the taste pleasant, makes it less inflame, and yet refresh the weak stomach with moderate heat and good relish.*

FYNES MORYSON • *ITINERARY*

## TOBACCO

*It makes your breath stink like the piss of a fox.*

THOMAS DEKKER • *THE HONEST WHORE*
ACT II SCENE II

Smoking tobacco has only become really popular within these last five years. It is smoked in small clay pipes. A filling can usually be bought at the theatre for 3 pence but the price by the pound varies enormously as there is as yet no certain source of regular supply.

*The habit is so common with them, that they ... light up on all occasions, at the play, in the taverns or elsewhere ... it makes them riotous and merry and rather drowsy, just as if they were drunk, though the effect soon passes – and they use it so abundantly because of the pleasure it gives, that their preachers cry out on them for their self-destruction and I am told the inside of one man's veins after death was found to be covered in soot just like a chimney.*

THOMAS PLATTER • 1599

# V · LAW AND ORDER

*Be Warned · Punishments · Men at Arms*

N<small>O ONE SHOULD BE SURPRISED THAT</small> London is the capital of crime. As England's biggest city by far it has more buildings to burgle, more goods to steal, more drunks to rob and more bemused visitors to deceive than anywhere else in the land.

Beggars desperate for their next crust account for much of the petty crime, but London has a large population of professional criminals, many of whom find refuge from the law in a dozen sanctuaries like St Martin's-le-Grand, the ruined buildings of the old Savoy Palace or Alsatia, or the area around the former Whitefriars monastery, between Fleet Street and the Strand. Here they can disappear into a maze of courts and alleys, knowing their neighbours will always obstruct or mislead anyone sent in pursuit of them. No honest citizen or prudent visitor would venture into these localities.

## BE WARNED

T<small>HE OFFENCES THAT ARE MOST LIKELY</small> to be committed against the unwary visitor are these:

**Theft** London's pickpockets and cutpurses are extraordinarily skilful. Thieves usually work in pairs or teams – one on the lookout for a likely victim,

perhaps another to distract him and a third to commit the actual theft. Often a ballad singer will gather a crowd and break off to warn spectators to look to their purses – which they immediately touch to reassure themselves, thus showing the singer's accomplice where they keep their cash. You are most at risk in crowded places, like St Paul's or the Royal Exchange, or at rowdy locations and occasions, like the playhouses, Bartholomew Fair and Lord Mayor's Day. Above all don't drink too

### LONDON LANGUAGE

*argent, bit, cross, lowre* – coin, cash
*brabble* – quarrel
*bong, bung* – purse, pocket
*broadsword* – heavy old-fashioned
sword for slashing rather than stabbing
*buckler* – small hand-held shield, now
outmoded
*cant, peddler's french* – criminal slang
*counterfeit crank* – rogue feigning
illness or disease
*cuttle* – knife
*foist* – sleight of hand at dice
*foister* – a pickpocket
*nipper* – a cutpurse
*shadow / stall* – accomplice of a foister
or nipper who identifies and
distracts victims

much. Drunks are easy victims in an alleyway or courtyard, especially in the dark.

*Confidence tricksters* One of the delights of a great city is to encounter so many different types of people, often with fascinating stories to tell. Beware tale-tellers appealing to you for charity. The most common ploys are those of the supposed sailor, who has lost all his possessions in a shipwreck ('freshwater mariner'), the gentleman fallen on hard times ('courtesy man'), the ex-soldier impoverished through service in a foreign war ('ruffler'), the pretended goodwife whose house has burned down ('demander for glimmer') and the fake priest pretending to beg alms for a hospital ('frater'). People who really have suffered these misfortunes or are genuinely collecting for a good cause will have an official printed licence to beg. Unfortunately in London, the centre of the printing trade, these are easily forged.

*Deception* Don't accept invitations to taverns, ordinaries or bowling alleys from people you don't know. Don't be persuaded to play cards, dice or tables with strangers. Don't let anyone hold your horse if you still expect it to be there when you turn round.

*Assault* The new fashion for carrying a rapier and dagger after the Italian manner has increased the number of serious stabbings. When men carried a broadsword and buckler these were usually impossible to use indoors or in a confined space. Going outside to

---

### LONDON LORE

Loaded dice (cheats, contraries) come in a variety of forms. They may be 'barred' so that they never turn up the 3 or 4 (cater-reys), 5 or 2 (cinque-deuces) or 6 or 1 (six-aces). Or they may be 'flat', which means they always turn up one of those combinations. 'Fullams' are corner-loaded to cast high (4–6) or low (1–3). A 'bum card' is one that is unobtrusively raised or marked for cheating purposes.

---

look for a suitable place for a fight often gave time for tempers to cool. But the cross-hilt dagger, worn at the back, is virtually a short sword, easily snatched out and lethal at close range.

### LAW ENFORCEMENT – CONSTABLES AND WATCHMEN

Watchmen patrol the streets at night, equipped with a stout staff and a lantern. Many are aged, infirm, disabled or otherwise incapable of other work. The watchmen are supervised by constables who are selected from the able-bodied householders of a parish and serve for at least a year. Serving as constable is a thankless task and those who have a good business to attend to are usually glad to pay another to take their place. The larger, richer parishes have at least a dozen or more watchmen, whose numbers make up a little for their feebleness. Poor, small parishes with few watchmen are therefore best avoided, especially at night. There are also professional informers and others who recover stolen goods – for a price.

## PRISONS

Considering that, with the exception of suspected conspirators against the throne, long terms of imprisonment are rarely imposed as a punishment, London is plentifully provided with places of incarceration.

Political prisoners go to the Tower of London. While some may expect to be closely confined and tortured, others, depending on their rank and the seriousness of the charge or weight of evidence against them, may live in some comfort, being allowed to have books, wine, good viands etc. sent in, to receive family and friends as visitors and to walk freely within the walls.

*Beware of the dog! Most ne'er-do-wells will be more wary of the dog than the watchman.*

LONDON LANGUAGE

*beak* – magistrate
*bellman* – nightwatchman
*catchpole, headborough* – arresting officer, constable
*derrick* – a hangman
*engines* – instruments of torture
*garnish* – bribe given to a prison officer
*law-day* – session of the Sheriff's court
*pettifogger* – legal practitioner dealing with minor offences
*pilliwinks* – torture device for pinching fingers
*shoulder-clapping* – arrest

The Marshalsea in Southwark, a private institution run for profit, has become second only to the Tower as an accommodation for royal prisoners. Newgate has the well-earned reputation of being even worse than most other prisons in terms of the danger of fever. Many awaiting trial die before ever coming before a judge. The Fleet prison, sited beside the river Fleet, is equally notorious for the abuse of inmates. Their treatment depends entirely on what they are able to pay. The Clink, a small lock-up on Bankside, usually holds disorderly patrons of the local brothels, which are controlled – rather surprisingly – by the Bishop of Winchester, who is the local landlord.

Bridewell, situated in a former palace built by Henry VIII, is mainly used for petty offenders who may be saved from a life of viciousness by a short, sharp

### LONDON LANGUAGE

*bawdy basket, callet, cockatrice, drab,*
*mistress o' the game, punk, quean,*
*singlewoman, stale, stewed prunes,*
*traffic, trug, winchester goose* – whore
*french marbles* – venereal disease
*occupy* – have sex with
*stew* – a brothel, originally
a steam-bath

period of correction – 'for the strumpet and idle person, for the rioter that consumeth all and for the vagabond that will abide in no place'. Floggings are administered twice a week. But inmates are also taught useful skills – 'in making of feather-bed ticks, wool-cards, drawing of wire, spinning, carding, knitting and winding of silk and other profitable devices'. They may, therefore, hope to find work upon their release. This institution has proved so successful that there are now additional Bridewells in Westminster and Clerkenwell, and others as far away as Norwich.

Ironically, prisons are often used as overnight refuges by thieves and harlots who, by paying 'garnish', can thus evade the watch.

## PUNISHMENTS

MANY PROFESSIONAL CRIMINALS have a sound working knowledge of the peculiarities of the English legal system, particularly with regard to punishment. If you can be induced to give me your horse to hold and I walk off with it, my punishment cannot exceed a fine of 40 shillings and a spell in the pillory, but if I break into your stables and steal it I hang.

*Beggars being whipped out of town at the cart's tail.*

Minor offences such as fornication and prostitution are punished by dragging the offender through the streets in a cart, with a placard about the neck naming their offence so they may be jeered at and spat on. Offences like selling short weight or stale goods usually merit a spell in the stocks, where the victims at least have their hands free and so can defend themselves against missiles. More serious offences, often involving violence, mean the pillory. In the pillory the miscreant has no chance of self-defence and can lose the sight of an eye, or have an ear nailed to the wood and then cut off. Offenders may also be branded on the cheek, hand or forehead so that honest citizens can be on their guard against them.

Death is the normal penalty for murder, manslaughter, treason, desertion from the battlefield, witchcraft, rape and robbery on the highway. Also for sodomy, stealing hawks and letting water out of ponds.

### TORTURE

In theory the English hate the idea of torture. In practice it occurs, particularly to extract information from suspected conspirators and Catholic priests. Usually the Privy Council has to give written authority to the torturers in the Tower of London. Here the victims may be cast into The Pit, a covered hole 20 ft deep into which no light enters, to lie there in their own filth. Another chamber, known as Little Ease, makes it

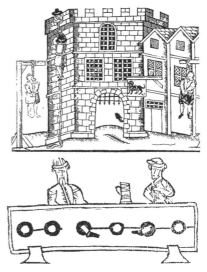

*Criminals are often punished near city gates for all to see the price of wrongdoing.*

impossible to stand upright or lie down. The Rack rips ligaments apart, causing indescribable pain and leaving its victims permanently crippled. The Scavenger's Daughter, an arrangement of fetters and irons, compresses the head, hands and feet to make the victim double up into a virtual ball, their muscles screaming for relief.

### EXECUTIONS

Executions in London serve as a free public spectacle, drawing an estimated one-third of the entire population onto the streets. Talk to almost anyone and they will be able to tell you the best places to stand. Get there early and don't worry about taking food or drink

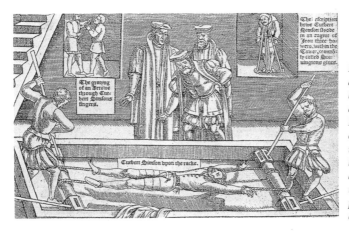

*The grating of an Iewe through Cutbert Simsons fingers.*

*Cutbert Simson vpon the racke.*

*The description howe Cutbert Simson stoode in an engine of Iron three houres, within the Colledge, commonly called Skee=uington gines.*

*Punishment is a public matter, but torture is a private affair. Pushed to extremes, the rack tears ligaments apart, leaving the victim permanently crippled.*

– there will be plenty of pedlars working the crowd. There will also be plenty of foisters and nippers working the crowd as well, so leave your valuables somewhere safe in your lodgings.

There are some 300 executions a year but no public executioner. Normally a butcher does the work. Apart from his fee, he has the right to sell lengths of the hanging rope, believed to be a powerful charm against illness. Hangings usually take place at Tyburn, to the west of the city and north of Westminster on the road to Oxford. Here there is a great gallows, with three arms, like a trivet, each arm being able to hang up to eight persons at once. The journey from Newgate is over 3 miles long and, thanks to the crowds all along the route, usually takes hours. The condemned criminal goes in a cart via the former leper hospital at St Giles-in-the-Fields, where, by custom, he drinks a large bowl of ale. At Tyburn the executioner puts a noose around his neck,

secures the end to the gallows and pulls the cart away, leaving the culprit to sway and kick until he finally chokes to death. With luck he may have bold friends to rush forward and hang onto his legs to break his neck.

Executions at Tower Hill are usually of nobility discovered in treasonous plots. In recognition of their status they are normally granted a swift death with the axe. Otherwise traitors face the extended agony of being hanged, drawn and quartered. The condemned person is hanged but kept conscious until the executioner slits him open from throat to privities, then pulls out his living heart before his face. After this he cuts off his head and quarters the body to be dragged through the streets of the city on a hurdle, before the head is spiked on London Bridge and the quarters nailed up over the gates of the city.

Pirates meet their end at Execution Dock, downriver at Wapping, where their bodies are left for the tide to wash over them three times, and are then suspended to act as a warning for every seaman. Heretics sentenced to death by burning may meet their fate either at Tyburn or outside the city walls at Smithfield. The fortunate ones choke to death from breathing in smoke before the flames can reach their bodies.

Sometimes executions occur where the criminal offence was committed. In 1586 Anthony Babington and his 13 confederates, who plotted the deposition of the Queen, were hanged, drawn and quartered in Lincoln's Inn Fields, near which they are supposed to have met to conspire. Anthony Middleton was a Catholic agent who was arrested at Clerkenwell and held for nine years for questioning, then executed on Clerkenwell Green.

Poisoning arouses special horror, as it usually occurs within a household at the hands of malicious servants or unnatural wives, husbands or children. In these latter cases it constitutes 'petty treason', a crime more heinous than common murder because it threatens the basic hierarchy of society. The punishments are burning at the stake or being boiled to death in water.

Suicides have a stake driven through the breast, their corpse exposed at a crossroads and then buried there, outside consecrated ground and trampled over by every passer-by.

Persons convicted of capital offences not only face the death penalty but also the forfeiture of all their property and goods to the Crown, leaving their family in destitution. This can be avoided by refusing to enter a plea of guilty or not guilty, remaining silent and opting to die by *peine forte et dure*, which means slowly dying of hunger and thirst while being pressed beneath heavy weights which are added to until it becomes impossible to breathe.

## MEN AT ARMS

ENGLAND HAS NO STANDING ARMY APART from the Queen's personal bodyguard and the garrisons of the Tower of London and various coastal fortresses. Because there has been no armed uprising in England itself these 30 years, combat experience must be sought

*Welcome to London. Traitors' heads adorn the gatehouse at the southern end of London Bridge.*

abroad. Many Englishmen have, therefore, fought for the Protestant cause as volunteers in the Netherlands or France or in the semi-permanent war in Ireland. If you are someone with military experience or, better still, expertise in artillery, engineering or fortification many gentlemen will be eager for your acquaintance and conversation, and likely to invite you to what will doubtless prove a memorable meal.

### THE ARTILLERY COMPANY

London's most prestigious military force is the Artillery Company, which was chartered by Henry VIII in 1537 as 'The Fraternity or Guild of Artillery of Longbows, Crossbows and Handguns'. Its main purpose is to supply officers for the trained bands (see below) and thus to contribute to the defence of London. Members have, however, also fought in foreign wars to gain experience and have served with the fleet against the Spanish Armada. The company has since become known as the 'Gentlemen of the Artillery Garden'. This refers to their practice and drill ground, which is on the east side of Bishopsgate. It is walled around for safety but you should have no trouble getting in if you are genuinely interested in watching.

### THE TRAINED BANDS

The trained bands are London's militia or citizen soldiers. Most are organized by the City Livery Companies, with separate units drawn from the Grocers, Drapers, Fishmongers etc. Most of the rank and file are younger men, hence journeymen and apprentices, rather than householders. They meet regularly in Finsbury Fields or on Mile End Waste to practise drill with pike and sword and every year are mustered for an inspection of their weapons and equipment. In terms of both they are held to be considerably better than the county militias, which look to them for a model. Elite units carry muskets, to the number of 4,000. On occasion the trained bands may be called out to keep order, as when apprentices threaten to become too rowdy on public holidays.

Many members of the trained bands are enthusiastic about their service. They certainly look smart. But after a day of drilling, they are used to taking a short stroll to the nearest tavern and then going home to a hot meal and a warm bed. How they would perform if they had to march any distance, spend nights under the stars and fight against experienced troops is another matter.

# VI · WHO'S WHO: PEOPLE WHO MATTER

*Men of the Moment · London's Leading Ladies*

M EN OF OUR TIMES THIRST FOR FAME and flock to London to find it, accompanied by their strong-willed and independently minded ladies. You may not get the chance to meet the most powerful of the people profiled here, but many of them can be seen along the Strand on their way to and from Court, when they will travel with an entourage – partly for security, but mainly to mark their rank and signal their importance. These prominent people are introduced here, as is only natural and to be expected, in order of their social standing. Inevitably this puts the actors and playwrights last in the male hierarchy, but one may at least be certain of seeing them or watching one of their plays for the price of entry to a theatre – a matter of pennies. As for the rest, if you never even catch a glimpse of them you will certainly hear Londoners talking about them.

## MEN OF THE MOMENT

### LORD HOWARD OF EFFINGHAM

The man who defeated the Armada still holds the post of Lord Admiral of England, as did his father and grandfather before him. The Lord Admiral holds

*Lord Howard is the third member of his illustrious line to serve as Lord Admiral.*

office for life and Charles Howard, Earl of Nottingham, looks fit to live forever. Even at 60 he commanded the expedition against Cadiz, totally defeating another Spanish fleet. A cousin of the Queen and a Garter Knight, he is married to Catherine Carey, one of the Queen's favourite ladies-in-waiting and the daughter of Lord Hunsdon. Howard has throughout a distinguished career won the respect and loyalty of finer seamen than himself, not least that eternal hero, the late Sir Francis Drake.

## ROBERT CECIL

*He had a full mind in an imperfect body ...
In a chair he had both a sweet and a grave
presence, as if nature understanding how
good a counsellor he would make, gave him
no more beauty of person anywhere else.*

SIR HENRY WOTTON

Robert Cecil has inherited the position of his father, the late Lord Burghley, as the Queen's closest confidant and most valued counsellor – and deservedly so. Despite being a small, stooping semi-invalid since birth, he was groomed for power and became a Member of Parliament at 21 and a member of the Privy Council before he was 30. As Chancellor of the Duchy of Lancaster, Cecil has extensive political patronage at his disposal. As principal Secretary of State he directs the foreign policy of the realm. As Master of the Court of Wards he occupies the single most remunerative office in government. Although he works himself unstintingly in the

*Right-hand man – Robert Cecil has succeeded to his father's position as the Queen's closest adviser.*

Queen's service, Cecil has broad interests and has begun to build a collection of paintings from all over Europe. He has made himself rich and has made numerous enemies, but at present his position seems unassailable.

### ROBERT DEVEREUX, EARL OF ESSEX

The Queen's favourite is also her cousin; he is stepson to her late favourite, Robert Dudley, Earl of Leicester, and as a child was the ward of Lord Burghley. Formidably intelligent, Essex was admitted to Cambridge at the age of 10. At 19 he fought at the battle of Zutphen, where his cousin, Sir Philip Sidney, the flower of English chivalry, was killed. Essex was created knight-banneret for his gallantry in the field and returned with Sidney's sword. The following year the Queen made him her

**LONDON LORE**

Ever mindful of his duty to the
common sailor, the Lord Admiral
has earned undying gratitude by
establishing 'The Chest at
Chatham', a fund for veterans
fallen on hard times.
He is also patron of the company
of actors known as the Lord Admiral's
Men, whose leading member is
Edward Alleyn.

Master of Horse and the year after that a Knight of the Garter, a remarkable token of favour from a sovereign noted for her parsimony with honours and titles. She has even forgiven him his marriage to Sidney's widow, which was kept secret from her at the time.

Essex is handsome, charming, extravagant, arrogant and short-tempered. In Ralegh he has a formidable rival, in Cecil an implacable enemy. Essex's decision to put his men ashore at Cadiz and raid the city brought him plunder and fame, but was in direct defiance of the orders of his commander, Lord Howard of Effingham. His attempt to capture the Spanish treasure fleet in the Azores was a fiasco. He has, nevertheless, been created Earl Marshal of England and Chancellor of the University of Cambridge. He has also been entrusted with command of a large and well-equipped expeditionary force to Ireland. Many a better general has floundered there and many hope Essex will flounder – and founder – in his turn.

*By God's death it were fitting some one should take him down and teach him manners!*

ELIZABETH I OF
THE EARL OF ESSEX

---

### SIR WALTER RALEGH

*What is our life? A play of passion,*
  *Our mirth the music of division,*
  *Our mothers' wombs the 'tiring houses be,*
  *Where we are dressed for this short Comedy,*

*Heaven the judicious sharp spectator is,*
*That sits and marks still who doth act amiss,*
*Our graves that hide us from the searching Sun,*
  *Are like drawn curtains when the play is done,*
  *Thus march we playing to our latest rest,*
  *Only we die in earnest, that's no jest.*

SIR WALTER RALEGH

Sir Walter Ralegh seems to be not one man but a court and company in

*The map in the background of Ralegh's portrait emphasizes his passion for colonization.*

himself – soldier, sailor, explorer, Member of Parliament, historian and poet. He calls himself Rawley and spells it Ralegh. Others spell it Raleigh and pronounce it Rally. Really!

When he was only 15 he fought as a volunteer in the Protestant cause in France. After a spell at Oxford he accompanied his half-brother, Sir Humphrey Gilbert, on his expedition against Spain. He later fought in Ireland. Between 1583 and 1589 Ralegh spent £40,000 on six expeditions to plant an English colony in America. All failed, perhaps in part because he had become so precious to the Queen that she forbade him to accompany any of them. Ralegh's personal expedition in search of the fabled city of gold, El Dorado, was likewise fruitless. The leading part he played in the raid on Cadiz has, however, restored him to favour at Court. Strangely, for such a cultured and courtly man, he has never lost – or attempted to lose – the broad Devon speech of a country squire. Enemies concede that he is a most accomplished linguist – except in English. Ralegh has a rapier wit, but not always sense to keep it in its scabbard. The Queen much enjoys his company but, though he has served as captain of her guards and on diplomatic missions, she has never entrusted him with domestic political office.

### SIR HORATIO PALAVICINO

Wherever there may be a profit you may be sure to find Sir Horatio

## LONDON LIVING

While exiled to the country Sir John Harington ingeniously devised what is called a 'water closet', which brings the convenience of an outdoor house of easement within one's own bedchamber but, he claims, without the attendant offensive odours. Her Majesty has recently commanded that a 'water closet' should be installed at Richmond Palace.

Palavicino, who has succeeded the late Sir Thomas Gresham as London's most prominent financier. Born in Genoa, he speaks six languages and could have made a fortune in any of half a dozen countries, but he has become a naturalized Englishman and a Protestant. Sir Horatio gets things done – buying foreign paintings and sculptures for connoisseurs, arranging the ransoms of Spanish prisoners of war, raising an army to invade France. He once loaned the Queen £29,000 – and received £41,000 back in interest payments alone. During famine times he has not scrupled to speculate in corn, to the acute distress of the poor. He has even tried to corner the world supply of pepper. Sir Horatio has bought up 8,000 acres over three counties and is said to be worth £100,000. He is cold, calculating, cruel and hated, close to the Cecils and an enemy of Essex.

### SIR JOHN HARINGTON

One of the Queen's 100 plus godsons, Sir John Harington owes his favoured place in her affection to his father's willingness 'to serve and love us in trouble and thrall'. When she was, as Princess Elizabeth, confined to the Tower of London, John Harington the elder conveyed a letter to her from friends outside and was fined £1,000 for it. The Queen never forgot this act of personal devotion, but Sir John the younger has frequently tried her patience. For translating a saucy story from Italian and circulating it among the maids of honour at Court, he was exiled to his estate near Bath. Since the incident Harington has been forgiven, banned again, forgiven again and banned again.

### DR JOHN DEE

Dr Dee lives in the shadows, rumoured to be a practitioner of dark arts. Over a decade ago his house at Mortlake, upstream from Westminster, was burned by a mob, who feared him as a magician or wizard. This cost him many precious manuscripts, rare books and scientific instruments. Dee is certainly expert on poisons, ciphers, alchemy and many other matters necessary for the secret conduct of the affairs of the state. It was

*Master of Arts. Dr John Dee, the Queen's magus.*

Dee who advised the Queen on the most auspicious date for her coronation. It was Dee who was sent for when a wax doll of Her Majesty, with a pin through its breast, was found in Lincoln's Inn Fields.

When Henry VIII founded Trinity College, Cambridge in 1546, Dee was made one of its original fellows, though not yet 20 years of age. He later studied at Louvain and Prague and lectured at Paris and is esteemed as a colleague by Europe's foremost scholars. John Stow, William Camden and Richard Hakluyt are proud to be numbered

*I cannot blot out from my memory's table the goodness of our sovereign Lady to me ... her watchings over my youth, her ... admiration of my little learning ... which I did so much cultivate on her command.*

SIR JOHN HARINGTON

among his friends. All the greatest English sea-captains – Frobisher, Gilbert, Drake and Ralegh – have turned to him for technical advice on gunnery and navigation. No stay-at-home scholastic, Dee has lived in Antwerp, Venice, Lorraine, Bohemia, Hungary and Poland and travelled as far as St Helena. Now in his 70s, Dr Dee has sired 11 children since he was 50 and remains upright, tall, slim and handsome, though his beard has turned milky white. Few of his many writings have been published, but he has given a new phrase to our language – 'the British Empire'.

### WILLIAM BYRD

William Byrd, an unrepentant Catholic, is still the most favoured musician of Her Majesty's Chapel Royal, protected from the usual consequences of his allegiance by the excellence of both his compositions and his performances. Byrd excels in all forms of music, sacred and secular, vocal and instrumental, and has written dozens of songs for solo voice and viol and over 100 pieces for the virginal. Despite his own religious allegiance he has composed unsurpassed Services and anthems for the liturgy of the Church of England – and possibly three Latin masses, said to have been published secretly. Byrd lives like a gentleman, in a manor house at the hamlet of Stondon Massey in Essex, near Brentwood, a day's ride eastwards from London.

This ease of living he owes to the favour of Her Majesty, who granted to him and to his teacher, the late Thomas Tallis, the sole right in the kingdom to publish printed music for over 20 years, from which they profited greatly. Byrd's fame stretches throughout Europe as the greatest musician that England has ever produced.

### NICHOLAS HILLIARD

*A hand, or eye, By Hilliard drawn, is worth an history, By a worse painter made.*

JOHN DONNE

Both goldsmith and limner to the Queen, Hilliard has won renown for his sublime skill in the painting of portraits in miniature, many of which he mounts in exquisite jewelled frames of

*A self-portrait of Nicholas Hilliard, who is on record as saying 'rare beauties are more commonly found in this isle of England than elsewhere'.*

his own devising. The paintings themselves are on vellum, mounted on card cut from playing cards. He has also designed and executed the Queen's Great Seal. Hilliard has in addition composed the definitive work on his field, a *Treatise concerning the Art of Limning*. Apart from the Queen herself, he has painted Sidney, Ralegh, Drake and numerous of the Queen's council. Other artists show the likeness of a sitter, Hilliard reveals the person.

> *Far to strange countries*
> *abroad his skill doth shine.*
> JOHN BALDWIN • 1591

---

### EDMUND SPENSER

---

> *At Delphos shrine, one did a doubt propound,*
> *Which by th'Oracle must be released,*
> *Whether of poets were the best renown'd:*
> *Those that survive, or they that are deceased?*
> *The Gods made answer by divine suggestion,*
> *While Spenser is alive, it is no question.*
>
> FRANCIS BEAUMONT
> ON MR EDM. SPENSER, FAMOUS POET

Edmund Spenser was translating Latin, French and Dutch into English verse before he even went up to Cambridge. The son of a London tradesman, Spenser was educated at the Merchant Taylors' School. His first major work, *The Shepherd's Calendar,* was composed while he was serving in the household of the late Earl of Leicester, and was dedicated to the late Sir Philip Sidney. Written in 12 sections, each in a different metre, the poem instantly established its author as the foremost poet of the age. For almost 20 years Spenser has served in the colonial administration in Ireland, but this wearisome task has not prevented him from completing his master work, *The Faerie Queen,* an epic allegory in praise of Her Majesty, which has won him a royal pension of £50 a year. This he most certainly needs, as Irish rebels have destroyed his castle and ravaged his estate, forcing him to return to London all but destitute. Among his losses were many poems never yet published – a loss also therefore to all who love the English language. Despite his long-standing friendship with Ralegh, Spenser also retains the affection and regard of Essex.

---

### RICHARD HAKLUYT

---

*Many of such useful tracts of sea adventures, which before were scattered as several ships, Mr Hakluyt hath embodied into a fleet, divided into three squadrons, so many several volumes; a work of great honour to England, it being possible that many ports and islands in America which being base and barren, bear only a name for the present, may prove rich places for the future.*

> THOMAS FULLER • THE HISTORY
> OF THE WORTHIES OF ENGLAND

A clergyman of the Church of England, Richard Hakluyt has made himself England's foremost authority on travel and exploration. While still in his 20s he became the first person ever to give a course of public lectures on geography at the University of Oxford. His first printed work, *Divers Voyages to America*, documented the Queen's title to newly discovered lands.

As chaplain to the English embassy in Paris, Hakluyt almost certainly served as an agent for the late Sir Francis Walsingham's espionage organization. The first volume of Hakluyt's best known work, *The Principal Navigations, Voyages, Traffiques and Discoveries of the English Nation*, was dedicated to Walsingham. The second volume was dedicated to Lord Howard of Effingham. Hakluyt is a protégé of Dr Dee and a vocal supporter of Ralegh's efforts to establish English colonies overseas. No study-bound pen-pusher, Hakluyt has proved himself a zealous ransacker of other men's memories, recording the experiences of the sea-captains of Bristol and St Malo, of former prisoners of the Spanish, of a ship's mate who had been to Florida and even of the Pretender to the throne of Portugal. Hakluyt believes England must be committed to expansion or go under.

> He [Alleyn] was the Roscius of our age, so acting to the life, that he made any part (especially a majestick one) to become him.
>
> THOMAS FULLER
> THE HISTORY OF
> THE WORTHIES OF ENGLAND

## EDWARD ALLEYN

Alleyn was acting by the age of 20 and by 25 was recognized as one of the four leading actors of the day, noted for his commanding stage presence and a voice of magnificent depth. He made his reputation playing the leading parts in Christopher Marlowe's *The Jew of Malta*, *Tamburlaine the Great* and *The Tragical History of Dr Faustus*. He made his fortune by marrying the daughter of Philip Henslowe, the proprietor of the Rose Theatre and a man with fingers in many profitable pies. Unlike his father-in-law, however, Alleyn has a well-deserved reputation for amiability and honesty as well as shrewdness. Together the two of them have prospered as bear-masters and property speculators, so much so that Alleyn may be contemplating permanent retirement from the stage. See him if – while – you can.

## RICHARD BURBAGE

If Alleyn has any real rival it is Richard Burbage, son of the proprietor of London's first purpose-built theatre, The Theatre at Shoreditch. Burbage made his stage debut as a boy. At Christmas in the year 1594 the Queen summoned Burbage and William Shakespeare to act before her at Greenwich. The two men have been closely associated ever since and have appeared before Her Majesty many times. Unlike Alleyn, Burbage is short and stout but nevertheless excels in tragedy and is renowned for the role of Richard III. It is no exaggeration to say that when presenting a new offering for the first time, every dramatist in London would have Burbage in the cast if he could. Unusually for a person so talented in one sphere, Burbage also shines in another, being a gifted painter in oils.

## WILLIAM SHAKESPEARE

*Some say (good Will) which I, in sport do sing,*
*Hadst thou not played some Kingly parts in sport,*
*Thou hadst been a companion for a King;*
*And, been a King among the meaner sort.*
*Some others rail; but, rail as they think fit,*
*Thou hast no railing, but, a reigning Wit.*

JOHN DAVIES • *THE SCOURGE OF FOLLY*

William Shakespeare can be said to have risen without trace. He was born, brought up and educated in Stratford-upon-Avon, a prosperous but small market town of some 1,500 people where his father has served as, in effect, the mayor, though not called that. Shakespeare's life between leaving his birthplace and arriving in London, a

*What did William Shakespeare do in the eight years between leaving Stratford and arriving in London?*

period of seven or eight years, remains a mysterious blank. Was he perhaps a member of a great man's household? Has he served as a soldier against the Spanish in the Netherlands? He seems to have a fascination with Italy – did he go there? Did he gain his first theatrical experience as a player of one-line parts with a strolling troupe? In truth, no one knows.

The first mention of Shakespeare in London is in a pamphlet written by Robert Greene in 1592, written on his deathbed. Greene's berating of the newcomer as an 'upstart crow' at least tells us that Master Shakespeare was not slow to make his mark among his fellow theatricals. It can only be imagined what Greene would have said about the fact that Shakespeare has since paid for a coat of arms for his father.

In the few years since he arrived in London William Shakespeare has shown himself to be a more than competent actor, an accomplished poet, a prolific dramatist and a budding man of business, already owner of the second largest house in Stratford-upon-Avon. In London he has moved from the parish of St Helen, Bishopsgate, over to Southwark to be near the new Globe Theatre, of which he is a part-owner.

Despite being no great scholar, Shakespeare seems to have an uncanny feeling for what will work on stage. He has already created a memorable villain in *Richard III*, a glorious hero in *Henry V*, fantastical fairies in *A Midsummer Night's Dream* and unforgettable doomed lovers in *Romeo and Juliet*. Remarkable for someone who, less than a decade ago, was said to be holding horses outside theatres, rather than looking to buy a share in one of his own. We shall doubtless hear much more from – and of – the Bard of Bankside, Master William Shakespeare.

*Ben Jonson's undeniable talents are at the mercy of his chaotic way of life.*

## BEN JONSON

Ben Jonson has already played many parts, some of them perilous. Despite being educated at Westminster School under the distinguished antiquarian William Camden, Jonson has done work as a bricklayer and fought as a volunteer in Flanders, where he killed a Spanish champion in single combat. Beginning as a strolling player, he soon became a playwright and was imprisoned for *The Isle of Dogs*, a satire 'containing very seditious and slanderous matter'. Jonson has also killed a fellow actor, Gabriel Spencer, in a duel, despite having a much shorter sword, and managed to get off with being branded as a felon rather than facing the rope. His first major play, *Every Man in his Humour*, included William Shakespeare, whom he much admires, in the cast. Almost all other of his fellow-playwrights he despises. Shakespeare returns the affection and regard and is said to have based Jaques in *As You Like It* on Jonson.

Jonson is himself much better as a dramatist than as an actor. In his person he is unclean and ill-favoured, his face pock-marked and with warts, his beard scraggy, his walk ungainly, his once slender figure inclining to a paunch. Jonson is often drunk and not infrequently so poor that he must live on bread and beans. He lives life on the edge and his future prospects are anyone's guess. He might become the darling of the Court – or die in the gutter.

## LONDON'S LEADING LADIES

*Elizabeth Hardwick, Countess of Shrewsbury* – 'Bess of Hardwick' – now comes down to London from Derbyshire only to consult her lawyers, but in her youth was a friend to the Queen when she was still a princess. Wed and widowed four times, this formidable old lady is reckoned to be the richest woman in England after the Queen herself. Having completed the building of a great house at Chatsworth, she has now built an even finer one, Hardwick Hall, which is more like a house of glass than of stone. Her life's purpose is now to secure the interests of her six children by her second husband, Sir William Cavendish, and thus she pursues an endless vendetta through the courts against her stepson, Gilbert Talbot (son of her last consort, the Earl of Shrewsbury) – who is married to one of her Cavendish daughters.

*Lady Elizabeth Hatton* is the granddaughter of Lord Burghley and when very young was married to the nephew and heir of Christopher Hatton, the Queen's celebrated 'Dancing Chan-cellor'. A wealthy widow at 20, she inherited Hatton House in Holborn and has since married the brilliant lawyer and Attorney General Edward Cooke. She has, however, rejected his name and, since the birth of their two daughters, has refused to live with him and even gives parties to which he is not admitted.

### LONDON LORE

In 1591 Bess left her Derbyshire fastness for her house in Chelsea, from which she raided retail London in a series of shopping expeditions to furnish Hardwick Hall. Her most expensive purchases were of tableware, consisting of gilt candlesticks, silver bowls and plates, cruets, cups, tankards and special vessels for sugar and salt. The other major outlay was on textiles, including 46 yards of velvet, 40 of satin, 50 of damask and 75 of linen for linings. Her single most expensive acquisition was a set of 17 tapestries telling the Biblical story of Gideon. These had originally been made for Sir Christopher Hatton, and cost £326. In just a matter of a few weeks the Countess managed to run up a total shopping bill of almost £800 – rather more than 50 years salary for a schoolmaster.

*Lucky Lucy.*
*Beautiful and brilliant, the*
*Countess of Bedford is reputed a*
*spendthrift but also, fortunately,*
*rich in her own right.*

**Catherine, Lady Howard,** is the daughter of the Queen's cousin, Lord Hunsdon, and the wife of the Lord High Admiral, the Earl of Nottingham. She has been one of the Queen's maids of honour since the beginning of her reign.

**Mary Herbert, Countess of Pembroke,** is the sister of the late Sir Philip Sidney and patron of many poets, most notably Edmund Spenser. She has herself translated both the Psalms and a French tragedy, *Antonius.*

**Lucy, Countess of Bedford,** married the third Earl when she was just 14. As yet unnoticed at Court, despite her beauty, she is a distant cousin of Sir Philip Sidney and evidently shares his poetic sensibility. She is educated, speaks French, Italian and Spanish and is a patron of the poets Michael Drayton and John Donne.

**Dorothy Percy, Countess of Northumberland,** is a sister of the Earl of Essex. When she was 18 she eloped with Sir Thomas Perrot and got married with two armed men guarding the door of the church to prevent any interruption. Since Perrot's death she has married the ninth Earl of Northumberland but does not live with him, spending most of her time at Essex House on the Strand.

**Elizabeth, Lady Ralegh** at 19 became maid of honour to the Queen and at 25 was married secretly to Sir Walter Ralegh. Their son was born clandestinely at the house of her brother, Arthur Throckmorton, at Mile End. When the Queen at last discovered the marriage, she sent both Elizabeth and Sir Walter to the Tower. Although Her Majesty relented after four months – perhaps on account of the death of the child – she has never forgiven Lady Ralegh's deceit and Lady Ralegh is not, therefore, received at Court. She resides consequently in Dorset most of the time but she makes occasional visits to London and has since borne another son, Walter.

**Margaret Ratcliffe,** maid of honour to the Queen, has this year died of grief and self-starvation on learning of the death of her brother Alexander in Ireland. Her burial in Westminster Abbey was attended by all of the Queen's ladies. Ben Jonson has written her epitaph and a poem of consolation to her father, a man doubly bereaved.

**Penelope Rich**, golden-haired and dark-eyed sister of the Earl of Essex, was the chosen beloved of Sir Philip Sidney, but was married off to the aged, ugly and very wealthy – and aptly named – Lord Rich, whose perjured evidence long ago cost Sir Thomas More his life. Sidney's love remained undimmed as he addressed sonnets to Penelope in the name of Stella. Since the death of Sidney she has become the mistress of the dashing soldier Charles Blount, Lord Mountjoy. She has had six children by Rich – and six more by Mountjoy.

**Anne Russell**, maid of honour to the Queen, is a great favourite, though two years ago she was briefly banished from Court for flirting with the Earl of Essex. She is engaged to marry Lord Herbert of Chepstow, the Queen herself promising to be present at the wedding with all her ladies.

**Elizabeth Wriothesley** (pronounced 'Rizley'), **Countess of Southampton**, is first cousin to the Earl of Essex and maid of honour to the Queen. She became pregnant by the Earl of Southampton, who secretly married her and was briefly sent to the Tower for it. While he was there Elizabeth fled to the home of Penelope Rich, where she had her baby, whom she named Penelope.

**Elizabeth, Lady Russell**, is another of those aged and litigious ladies who busies herself with ordering the lives of her offspring. She had two sons by her first husband, one posthumously, and two daughters by her second, though she was 46 when she married him. The first, Bess, is the Queen's godchild, the second, Anne, is to marry Lord Herbert. Although she lives mainly in the country Lady Russell keeps a town house in Blackfriars and was one of the leading petitioners who successfully prevented James Burbage from turning his local rehearsal rooms into a public playhouse. She bombards her nephew, Robert Cecil, with petitions on behalf of her many protégés, but he ignores them, likewise her pleas for support in her legal wrangle with Lord Admiral Howard over the custodianship of Donnington Castle, which the Queen bestowed on her in violation of his rights.

# VII · MUST-SEE SIGHTS

*London Bridge · Tower of London · London Stone*
*The Royal Exchange · Guildhall · St Paul's Cathedral*
*Somerset House · Whitehall · St James's Palace*
*Westminster Abbey · Westminster Hall · The River Thames*

WHATEVER YOUR PURPOSE IN COMING to London, you must make time for the major city sights that Londoners themselves so often take for granted. If you're arriving from the south you will enter over London Bridge – it's the only one linking the main part of the city, on the north bank, with the suburb of Southwark on the south. If your interest centres on the Court, you will make your way to the palaces of Whitehall and St James's; but be aware that the Privy Council often meets at Somerset House. If you're here for business, this centres on the Royal Exchange – though remember that the city is governed from Guildhall and the major law courts are to be found in Westminster Hall. On Sunday you may choose to worship either in Westminster Abbey or St Paul's Cathedral or any of more than a hundred parish churches; but for the best sermons go to Paul's Cross. You should allow at least half a day for the Tower – the rest according to your interests. The following check-list, after London Bridge, runs from east to west.

> DAVY: *'I hope to see London once ere I die.'*
> WILLIAM SHAKESPEARE
> *HENRY IV PART II*
> *ACT V SCENE III*

---

## LONDON LORE

Stow records that in 1536, a maid in the London Bridge household of the weaver William Hewett was playing at a window with his baby daughter, Anne, and let her fall into the river. Edward Osborn, Hewett's apprentice, dived straight in and rescued the infant. By the time Anne was old enough to be married Hewett, who had become very rich, refused all other suitors but Osborn, giving him both his daughter and a huge dowry. Hewett went on to become Lord Mayor – and so did Osborn.

---

## LONDON BRIDGE

LONDON BRIDGE, ONE OF THE WONDERS of Europe, was completed almost four centuries ago. Lined with over a hundred houses and shops, it once even had a chapel. Small islands of rocks and brushwood called 'starlings' protect the stone arches. These narrow the gaps between them to produce a dangerous flood like a mill-race every time the tide turns. The young – and foolish – like to shoot these rapids in a boat, but the outcome can be fatal. Be warned.

Crossing over the bridge can itself be quite a challenge. Unless you have hired

*City of a hundred spires. London Bridge, flanked by the church of St Mary Overie, William Shakespeare's church. Nonsuch House is at the centre of the picture.*

a local steed used to the traffic you would be well advised to lead your horse rather than try to ride it through the throng of carts, riders, shoppers, loiterers, beggars, sheep, cattle and stray dogs. But whether you walk or ride, do keep to the left, as you would on the open road.

Towards the southern end of the bridge, over the seventh and eighth arches, stands Nonsuch House, which projects over the river on both sides. This masterpiece of the woodworker's art, four storeys high, astonishes the onlooker with its domes and gables, galleries and turrets, all richly carved and gilded.

*London Bridge was made for wise men to pass over and for fools to pass under.*

ENGLISH PROVERB

The whole house was made in pieces in Holland and brought over by ship to be put together with wooden pegs; there is not a nail in the entire building.

At the southern end of the bridge, you can see the heads of traitors, usually about 20 or 30 of them, displayed on stakes. Only those of noble birth or great eminence suffer this fate and, astonishingly, some of the foremost among the nobility of today actually boast that their ancestors had this curious 'honour'. This is to prove that their bloodline brought them close enough to the throne to encourage them to try to take it for themselves.

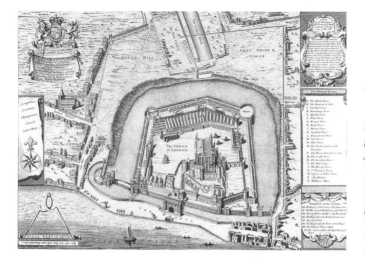

*Her Majesty's palace and fortress, the Tower of London. Once herself a prisoner, the Queen works, but does not live, here.*

## THE TOWER OF LONDON

*A most famous and goodly citadel, encompassed round with thick and strong walls, full of lofty and stately turrets, fenced with a broad and deep ditch, furnished also with an armoury or magazine of warlike munitions, and other buildings besides; so as it resembles a big town.*

WILLIAM CAMDEN • *BRITANNIA* • 1586

The Tower of London is one of those places you will be fascinated to visit – and relieved to know that you can leave at the end of your tour. It stands to the east of London Bridge and was built both to protect the bridge from attack and to dominate the eastern side of the city. The name of '*the* Tower' is misleading because there are 20 towers, not just one. At the centre is a high keep known as the White Tower and surrounding it are two circuits of wall, set with the other towers, which serve variously as strongpoints, storehouses and prisons. Londoners will tell you that the Tower was built by Julius Caesar, but Stow is sure that it was the work of 'William I, surnamed Conqueror'.

Stow also summarizes the many purposes the Tower serves:

*This tower is … to defend or command the city: a royal place for assemblies and treaties; a prison of estate for the most dangerous offenders: the only place of coinage for all England at this time: the armoury for warlike provision: the treasury of the ornaments and jewels of the crown: and general conserver of the records of the King's courts of justice at Westminster.*

*THE TOWER TOUR*

Guardsmen of the garrison conduct regular tours of the Tower. In the armoury you can handle the actual helmet, shield, armour and mace used by the late King Henry VIII. Nothing else could prove so clearly that he really was a giant of a man. A tip of 3 English shillings is usual for the keeper of the armour. In the next room are the king's guns (another tip is payable). A different room has a huge store of bows and arrows and yet another holds spears and saddles (third tip). The artillery includes a gun with seven barrels (tip expected). You will be told that everything not made for the king's use or on his orders was captured from England's enemies.

After the dining hall and guard room you can see the dungeon with its rack and other terrible instruments of torture. For many poor devils it was enough just to show them the thumbscrews and pincers and pokers and let their imagination do the rest, so that they willingly confessed to any crime or conspiracy. Doubtless most were, indeed, guilty – but spare a thought for the innocent, who were terrified into lying their lives away – English Jesuits and many a good Catholic gentleman whose only crime was to be torn between faith and country. But any threat to the life of the Queen justifies the sternest measures.

When you pass on to the next suite of rooms, it's another world – the

**LONDON LORE**

Some Germans who worked at the Mint in the Tower of London became ill through breathing in the noxious fumes given off from the molten metal they were handling. A physician advised them that they might be cured by drinking from a dead man's skull. The Aldermen responsible for the Mint therefore got a warrant from the Council to take some of the heads from London Bridge and make them into cups – 'whereof they drank and found some relief, though most of them died'.

*One of the superb jousting armours to be seen on display at the Tower.*

## LONDON LORE

When she was still a princess, Queen Elizabeth was sent to the Tower in March 1554 on the orders of her sister, Queen Mary. Exhaustive enquiries failed to uncover any evidence of Elizabeth's involvement in plots against Mary and she was released in May. When Mary died in 1558 and Elizabeth entered London as Queen, she rode to the Tower, patted the ground and said 'Some have fallen from being princes of this land to be prisoners in this place. I am raised from being prisoner in this place to be prince of the land.'

chamber used by the Queen in council dazzles the onlooker with splendid tapestries and cushions embroidered with pearls and precious stones. Beyond, in a further room, is a tapestry said to be 500 years old (fifth tip).

From the roof of the White Tower you get a panoramic view of the shipping which crowds the river from one side to the other (tip). Other highlights of great interest are watching gold and silver coins being minted (tip) and seeing the beasts of the royal menagerie. These include lions (which appear on the royal coat of arms), a tiger, a lynx, a porcupine and, supposedly, the last wolf left in England. (A final gratuity is payable here.) The standard tour does not include a viewing of the royal crown and jewels – for which a separate fee should be agreed.

The number of tips extorted from visitors is indeed excessive, but the guards think foreigners are fair game. A good 'tip' for the visitor is to go with a Londoner, dress like a local, literally play dumb and let him do the talking. Better still, head east outside the walls to the 'Tower Hamlets' from which the garrison is recruited. Catch one of the guardsmen off duty in an alehouse and you may well get your tour for the price of a jug – and the promise of several more afterwards.

## LONDON STONE

*On the south side of this High Street ... is pitched upright a great stone ... fixed in the ground very deep, fastened with bars of iron and otherwise so strongly set that if carts do run against it through negligence the wheels be broken and the stone itself unshaken.*

JOHN STOW • *A SURVAY OF LONDON* • 1598

This London landmark on Candlewick Street, running parallel with the river, is chiefly renowned just for being old. Rounded and rough and about the size of two large loaves on top of one another, it has a shallow groove along the top. There are no inscriptions. Some think the Romans measured distances to London from this point. But no one knows for certain what it was for. Londoners venerate it, not as a sacred thing, but simply because it is *very* old. If you are passing, it's worth pausing to see, but not a special visit.

## THE ROYAL EXCHANGE

THIS WONDERFUL BUILDING DOMI-
nates the western end of Cornhill
where it joins Cheapside, and stands at
the heart of London proper as the focal
point of its business life. The Exchange
was the gift of Sir Thomas Gresham,
based on the Bourse at Antwerp where
merchants meet to do business.
According to Stow, the traditional
meeting place for this used to be
Lombard Street: 'The merchants and
tradesmen, as well English as strangers,
for their general making of bargains,
contracts and commerce, did usually
meet twice every day. But these meet-
ings were unpleasant and troublesome,
by reason of walking and talking in an
open street, being there constrained to
all extremes of weather, or else to shelter themselves in shops.'
Completed in 1567, the Exchange
stands four storeys high and has a bell-
tower topped by a huge grasshopper, an
emblem from the Gresham crest. On
summer Sundays at 4 o'clock a free
concert of music may be heard playing
from the bell-tower. Merchants do
their trade on the ground floor, which
can accommodate up to 4,000 at a
time. In January 1570 the Queen dined
with Sir Thomas and then ordered her-
alds and trumpeters to proclaim that
henceforth his Bourse should be
known as 'The Royal Exchange'.

Three dozen houses were torn down
to clear the site for the new Exchange
and all the main materials for its building were brought from the Low
Countries – bricks from Antwerp,
slates from Dort and the wainscot and
glazing from Amsterdam. The archi-
tect, the masons and even the labourers
were also brought over from Flanders.
As one might imagine, this did not sit
well with the Worshipful Companies of
Masons, Carpenters and Glaziers, but

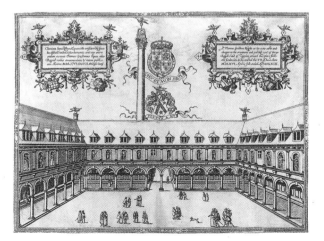

*The Royal
Exchange is the
hub of London's
commercial life –
this is a quiet day.*

*The present cathedral is the fourth St Paul's to stand on the low hill that dominates the city.*

Sir Thomas was adamant that only what was good enough for Antwerp was good enough for London. The irony is, of course, that Antwerp was taken and sacked by the Spanish in 1585 and the population of that city was halved in less than five years. So, if you want to see what the Antwerp Exchange looked like in its days of glory – come to London.

## GUILDHALL

GUILDHALL, A LOFTY STONE STRUCTURE, stands west and north of the Royal Exchange and is where the Lord Mayor and Aldermen order London's affairs and entertain royalty or important foreign guests. Guildhall is also used for state trials for heresy or treason, as in the case of Lady Jane Grey for falsely accepting the throne, and Archbishop Cranmer for refusing to renounce his Protestant faith.

Inside Guildhall are statues of Gogmagog and Corineus, representatives of the race of giants said to people these islands before the descendants of the Trojans came to found London as 'New Troy'. You can see also these statues carried in the procession on Lord Mayor's Day.

## ST PAUL'S CATHEDRAL

THIS IMMENSE CHURCH STILL LOOMS over the western half of the city, even though the spire was destroyed by fire after being struck by lightning in 1561. The main part of the building dates from the reign of Henry III. Its greatest glory is an immense rose window of brilliantly coloured stained glass. When the rays of the setting sun shine through it, it bathes the interior of the church with the hues of a dozen rainbows.

The nave of the cathedral has become a common thoroughfare, known as Paul's Walk. Londoners use it as a shortcut between Paternoster Row to the north and Carter Lane to the south. Here you see street sellers passing through with jugs of ale, trays of pies and pasties and baskets of fruit. Men even lead horses and mules through. People throng here to do all kinds of business. Tradesmen use tombs as shop counters. On either side of Paul's Walk servants looking for a new master come here to be hired, and lawyers and money-lenders receive their clients. Public lotteries are drawn at the west door.

According to the playwright Thomas Dekker, the cathedral has become such a haunt of the fashionable that tailors lurk behind pillars to take notes on the cut and colour of the newest garments made up by their rivals. On Sunday evenings in summer, men and women come to catch the cool air by paying a penny each to stroll on the roof of the cathedral, which is covered with lead. Dekker advises that 'before you come down again I would desire you to draw your knife and grave your name ... so you shall be sure to have your name lie in a coffin of lead, when yourself shall be wrapped in a winding sheet'.

Despite the casual way with which Londoners treat their cathedral, the Queen often attends services here and does not scruple to interrupt a sermon if it does not please her. In 1588 she came to St Paul's in great triumph to receive dozens of banners captured from the defeated ships of the Spanish Armada.

## PAUL'S CROSS

This celebrated preaching place stands immediately to the north of the cathedral, at its eastern end. The wooden pulpit has a lead roof and the most learned divines may be heard here. Royal proclamations, foreign news and public notices of processions, feasts and plague precautions are also read out here and forbidden books publicly burned. Sermons usually last at least two hours, measured by the glass. Preachers have bread and wine to sustain themselves and their voices, and afterwards take lunch with the Lord Mayor. The space around the cross accommodates upwards of 5,000 listeners, almost twice as many as any theatre. If it rains the preacher adjourns to the crypt of the cathedral.

## SOMERSET HOUSE

*That large and beautiful house, but yet unfinished.*

JOHN STOW • *A SURVAY OF LONDON* • 1598

Somerset House stands at the eastern end of the Strand, which leads towards Whitehall. It is the first palace in England in the Italian style, with a gateway of three storeys flanked by a symmetrical façade of two storeys and, inside, a courtyard with an entirely new feature called an arcade – a sort of tunnel of columns but with one side open. The builder was the Duke of Somerset, the uncle of Edward VI and Lord Protector of the realm. To clear the site he had several bishops' and lawyers' inns and a church torn down, and used stone from the priory of the Knights Hospitaller at Clerkenwell for the actual building. After the duke was beheaded for treason, the house was given to the Queen, who was then still a princess. Much of the building has been divided into apartments for foreign ambassadors and for royal favourites, like Lord Hunsdon, the commander of the Queen's bodyguard.

## WHITEHALL

WHITEHALL, THE MAIN LONDON palace of the Queen, was first built by Cardinal Wolsey, chief minister

to Henry VIII, who seized it for himself when Wolsey was disgraced. A road runs right through it, parallel to the river and spanned by two great gatehouses. This enables the visitor to pass from end to end, catching many glimpses of the interior. Titled foreigners may, on application, tour the state apartments under escort. Providing the Queen herself is not actually in residence, lesser mortals can usually see parts of the palace by tipping the appropriate door-keepers.

The buildings and apartments facing onto the Thames are chiefly for purposes of state, while those on the other side, facing onto the hunting park, are chiefly for pleasure. Because England had been at peace for almost 40 years when Cardinal Wolsey began to extend the old London residence of the Archbishop of York into a princely dwelling, Whitehall is not fortified.

*You must no more call it York Place; that's past, For since the Cardinal fell, that title's lost 'Tis now the King's and called Whitehall.*

WILLIAM SHAKESPEARE
*HENRY VIII*

*Whitehall, like most palaces, lies alongside London's main artery, the Thames.*

King Henry added gardens and orchards, tennis courts, a cockpit and a tilt-yard for jousting. When the Queen wishes to hear a play the actors use the Great Hall. Whitehall is said to have some 2,000 rooms, and some claim it as the biggest palace in all Europe, more like a village than a building. It is not beautiful, being a confusion of many styles. Nevertheless, it houses the greatest collection of international art in the realm.

## ST JAMES'S PALACE

O N THE FAR SIDE OF THE PARK FROM Whitehall stands St James's Palace, which was built by King Henry VIII on the site of a former leper hospital. It was essentially for use as a hunting lodge, but has since been used for holding court. It is said that no flowers will grow in the grounds round about because so many lepers have been buried there. Queen Mary, late sister to the present Queen, died at St James's. To the right of the imposing turreted gatehouse you will see the large window of the Chapel Royal. It is well worth waiting there whenever its choir is rehearsing or performing, just to catch even a snatch of the music.

## WESTMINSTER ABBEY

WESTMINSTER ABBEY, THE WORK OF many centuries, lies at the western extremity of the city and its suburbs. Dedicated to St Peter, it is the coronation church and main burial place of England's kings and queens. The nave is over 100 ft high, far higher than any other church in the country. Every sovereign since William the Conqueror has been crowned here.

The visitor can see the tombs and effigies of Edward the Confessor, Edward I, Edward III, Richard II, Henry V, Henry VII, Queen Mary and Edward VI. At the tomb of Henry V you can still see the actual shield, sword and helmet he had at his great victory over the French at Agincourt. In the gallery above lies the embalmed corpse of his French bride, Queen Katherine of Troyes, in an open coffin.

Since the Reformation of the English Church the former chantry chapels have become a fashionable place of burial for courtiers and members of the nobility. The most spectacular monument in the entire abbey, 36 ft high, commemorates Henry Carey, Lord Hunsdon, in the chapel of St John the Baptist. A great jouster in his youth, he was the Queen's

Parliament House · the Hall · the Abby

cousin and served her as Lord Chamberlain and Privy Councillor.

You can buy a printed guide to the monuments of abbey, in Latin.

## WESTMINSTER HALL

T HIS IS THE OLDEST SURVIVING PART OF the palace of Westminster, first built by Edward the Confessor. The remarkable roof rises over 90 ft above the floor and has the widest span in the country. It covers half an acre, weighs 660 tons and was made over 200 years ago at Farnham, 30 miles away, and brought in sections by cart and barge. Westminster Hall is home to the most important law courts – Queen's Bench, Common Pleas and Exchequer. After coronations the celebratory banquet is held here. On these occasions the Royal Champion, an office hereditary in the Dymoke family, rides to the centre of the Hall in full armour and requires that any man challenging the new sovereign's right to the throne shall meet him in single combat. No one ever has.

*Westminster, the setting for counsel, courts and coronations.*

And, finally, don't forget …

## THE RIVER THAMES

*The river was full of tame swans, who have nests and breed on small islands … They are exclusively used for the Queen's table and it is on pain of death forbidden to meddle with them.*

LUPOLD VON WEDEL · 1585

*A man would say, that seeth the shipping there, that it is, as it were, a very wood of trees disbranched to make glades and let in light, so shaded it is with masts and sails.*

WILLIAM CAMDEN · BRITANNIA · 1586

*I would here make mention of … the two thousand … small boats, whereby three thousand poor watermen are maintained … beside those huge… boats and barges which either carry passengers or bring necessary provision from all quarters.*

WILLIAM HARRISON
DESCRIPTION OF ENGLAND · 1587

# VIII · SHOPPING

*What to Buy · How to Buy It · Where to Shop*
*Markets · Fashion*

## WHAT TO BUY

IN LONDON YOU CAN BUY WHAT CANNOT BE bought elsewhere, not merely the necessities and conveniences of life but whatever is newest, most curious, most splendid or rarest. Staple items of London's luxury trades include guns, swords, armour, clocks, mirrors, books, maps, musical instruments, navigational and scientific instruments, spectacles, glassware, jewelry and plate, spices, drugs, furs and every kind of cloth and clothing you can imagine. English embroidery is particularly fine, whether applied to household items, like wall hangings, or items of apparel, notably gloves. Thus it makes an ideal gift to take home with you for any female who appreciates exquisite needlework – easily packed, lightweight and unlikely to get damaged in transit.

## HOW TO BUY IT

AS A VISITOR YOU MAY FIND SHOPPING is made considerably more complicated by the local systems of weights and measures – which vary according to the product being sold.

A penny will always buy a loaf – but the weight of a penny loaf varies with the price of grain. English-made cloth is usually sold by the ell. To Flemish visitors this means the equivalent of 27 English inches, to the Scot a shade over 10 inches longer than that. For the English, however, an ell equals 45 inches. Imported cloths, like satins, are sold by

### LONDON LANGUAGE

*bombast* – wadding used to stuff doublets and breeches
*cheapen* – bargain for
*cordwainer* – worker in the best leather, originally imported from Córdoba
*costermonger* – stallholder, especially selling fruit, from costard, a type of large apple
*currier* – craftsmen who turns skins into leather
*farthingale* – hooped frame around the waist from which the skirt is draped
*galligaskins / gallislops / gascoins* – baggy breeches, especially as worn by sailors
*head-tire* – head-dress consisting of a wire support and decorative covering of jewels, feathers, false hair etc.
*merchants by the great* – wholesalers
*plumping* – padding
*pomander* – ballot containing sweet-smelling herbs
*purl* – an embroidered border
*quietus* – settlement of an account
*trull* – person of low character
*ware-bench* – shop counter

*Check under the counter – the best produce is not always on show. Don't be afraid to ask for exactly what you want.*

the yard. Unlike other types of cloth, silk goes by weight, at approximately 2 shillings and 8 pence the ounce. Writing paper comes by the quire, which means 24 sheets (usually about 4 pence) – but sometimes 25.

When shopping, therefore, it clearly helps to be accompanied by a local who understands these matters.

## WHERE TO SHOP

### *ST PAUL'S CHURCHYARD*

London, Oxford and Cambridge have a monopoly on printing throughout the land, with London by far the greatest centre. Printers, many of them Flemings and Frenchmen as well as English, may be found on and around Fleet Street but the centre of the trade for binding and selling books lies around the churchyard of St Paul's Cathedral. This area gets especially busy during the four law terms when litigants and lawyers alike take the opportunity to combine courtroom combat with loosening the strings of their purses to buy books for both recreation and reference. Here you can purchase handsome, heavy volumes bound in the finest Morocco or, for mere pennies, any number of pamphlets, ballads and almanacs. When buying books unbound expect to pay 2 pence for three or four printed sheets.

Some current prices:

Holinshed's *Chronicles* – 26 shillings
Latin Testament – 2 shillings
Bible – 6 shillings
Camden's *Britannia* – 5 shillings
Hakluyt's *Principal Navigations* – 11 shillings and 11 pence
Shakespeare's *Venus and Adonis* – 1 shilling

### *CHEAPSIDE*

A small gate leads out from St Paul's churchyard onto Cheapside, which is the broadest street in London, wide enough for parades, pageants and processions, not to mention executions and even jousts.

The main side streets specialize in different trades. The bakers are on Bread Street, the fishmongers on Friday Street, shoemakers and curriers of leather on Cordwainer Street, dairymen in Milk Street and grocers in Sopers Lane. At the west end of Cheapside are saddlers and a market-house for corn and meal. At the east end there are cutlers and then the street becomes known as Poultry, where chickens and geese and pigeons are sold. Down the middle of Cheapside runs a street market where those passing through can buy flowers, fruit or tarts and pies. Part is reserved for sellers coming in from the countryside, bringing bread from Stratford, cheese cakes from Islington and vegetables from Hackney.

The finest section of Cheapside is Goldsmiths' Row, between Bread Street and Friday Street. This is enthusiastically described by Stow as 'the most beautiful frame of fair houses and shops that be within the walls of London or elsewhere in England … It containeth … ten fair dwelling houses and fourteen shops, all in one frame uniformly builded four storeys high, beautified towards the street with the Goldsmiths' Arms and … richly painted over and gilt.'

---

### LONDON LIVING

Some current prices of everyday household items:

3 brooms – 2 pence
1 pound of candles – 4 pence
1 pound of soap – 4 pence
6 spoons – 5 pence
Glass bottle – 1 shilling
12 pewter trenchers – 5 shillings
Looking-glass – 5 shillings

---

At the western end of Cheapside is the Liberty of St Martin's-le-Grand. This is now the name of the area's main street, but was once the name of the monastery which stood here from Saxon times. Many foreign craftsmen live here, making jewelry – much of it, according to the Worshipful Company of Goldsmiths, clearly counterfeit – but the area is an ancient sanctuary for ne'er-do-wells, outside the jurisdiction of the Lord Mayor, and enforcing proper trading standards there has always been a headache.

On the north side of Cheapside stands the hall of the Worshipful Company of Mercers. Therefore many of the nearby shops are those of mercers, iridescent with gorgeous silks, satins, velvets and other finery. *Very* tempting. The best way to take your wife through here is in a carriage with the blinds drawn down. As you drive past the side street called Bucklersbury she can easily be distracted by the amazing aromas escaping from the apothecaries' shops.

---

### THE ROYAL EXCHANGE

The Royal Exchange stands at the eastern end of Cheapside, beyond Poultry. Its upper galleries are crowded with over 150 small outlets selling everything from millinery to mousetraps. The rents from these retail outlets go to support the professors of Gresham College. The Exchange is conspicuously free from beggars, but beware of pickpockets here. If buying for you is a bore and a chore at least this is the place for one-stop shopping to get it over with quickly. But if your purse is itching for retail relaxation it's a purchasing paradise.

## THE STRAND

The Strand is a grand riverside thoroughfare leading from Fleet Street to Charing Cross and Westminster. The south side is lined with the mansions of the aristocracy, facing towards the river, but between them and along the northern side of the Strand more and more shops are being established, some to supply the residences of the rich, others to tempt the constant flow of passers-by.

## MARKETS

THE MAIN MARKETS FOR DAILY PROvisions are as follows:

Leadenhall, on the east side of Gracechurch Street, near its junction with Cornhill, is a main market for meat and poultry, with permanent London butchers' stalls in a stout stone building. For the serious trencherman.

Gracechurch Street is for country sellers of butter, cheese, whey, rabbits, piglets, pigs' heads, sausages and whatever may be easily carried there in a basket. Before they sell it you should smell it.

Eastcheap, to the south, nearer the river, is a street market for London butchers, with slaughterhouses nearby.

There is another meat market along Newgate Street near Smithfield, where live animals are sold on Wednesdays and Fridays. Wholesale only. Recommended only if you're planning to feed the 5,000.

Billingsgate, on the river, south of Eastcheap, sells fish, fruit, grain and salt fresh from France. A day trip to Calais without the dawn start or that bothersome voyage.

Stocks Market takes its name from the stocks where petty offenders are confined for punishment. There are stalls for about 20 each of butchers and fishmongers, all Londoners. For long-stay residents who want to cultivate their own 'little man round the corner'.

Queenhithe, right on the river, south of the Stocks Market, has a market

### LONDON LIVING

The market inspectors must be constantly vigilant against malpractice. Some poultry sellers, for example, sew up the vents of their birds days before their sale so that they swell out with the retention of their dung, seeming bigger and weightier than they really are. By the time the buyer comes to cook their purchase it is already too diseased to be edible and must be thrown away. The London poulterers with regular stalls know that they would be immediately open to complaint and would not practise such a low trick, but country incomers well might.

*Eastcheap market. Whatever it is, if English merchants can get it on to a ship, you can get it when you shop.*

house for the sale of fruit and grain brought by boat from upstream. This is as fresh as it gets. When others' produce begins to wilt, Queenhithe's won't!

On the south side of the river, in Southwark, along the approach road to London Bridge, there is a general market four times a week where both Londoners and country folk may sell. Convenient for picking up nuncheon on the way to the theatre, or ingredients for supper on the way back.

### PROTECTING THE CUSTOMER

The lord mayor and his officers supervise all the markets and have the power to control prices and confiscate unfit goods and produce. All scales and measures are officially checked, with standard weights kept in Guildhall to test them against. Markets are supposed to be open every day except Sunday, from 6 until 11 o'clock in the morning and from 1 until 5 o'clock in the afternoon. On Sundays milk, fruit and vegetables may be bought before 7 o'clock in summer, 8 o'clock in winter. Bread must either be purchased from the baker's premises or sold house to house from a basket, but not on the streets. Providing they keep moving, sellers of fish, oysters, cherries, strawberries, radishes, lettuces, wafers and other such items that are best got freshest, may sell their goods from a basket or pannier. Because mackerel goes off so quickly, you can buy it even on a Sunday.

### FASHION

*What shall I say of their doublets ... full of jags and cuts and sleeves of sundry colours? Their galligaskins to bear out their bums and make their attire to fit plum round (as they term it) about them? Their farthingales, and diversely coloured nether stocks of silk, jersey and such like, whereby their bodies are rather deformed than commended? I have met with some of these trulls in London so disguised that it hath passed my skill to discern whether they were men or women.*

WILLIAM HARRISON
*DESCRIPTION OF ENGLAND* • 1587

In theory what one may wear is governed by 'Acts of Apparel', detailed regulations with the force of law. Thus only Knights of the Garter and persons of the rank of Earl and above, for example, are supposed to wear cloth of gold or silver or purple silk. There are exemptions for gentlemen actually in attendance on the Queen or serving on a foreign embassy or having a disposable income of at least £200 a year. In practice, outside the royal court, these rules are widely ignored.

## MENSWEAR

*No people in the world is so curious in new fangles as they of England be … it is very hard to know who is noble, who is worshipful, who is a gentleman and who is not.*

PHILIP STUBBES • *THE ANATOMY OF ABUSES*

Men's doublets are stuffed and padded so that one can scarcely move in one, though having detachable sleeves makes this easier. Over this comes a jerkin, often lined but neither padded nor stiffened. On top of this is worn a

---

### LONDON LIVING

Fashion costs:

pair of workman's boots – 1 shilling

workman's shirt – 2 shillings

making up two coats and two pairs
of breeches – 5 shillings

pair of fashionable
summer boots – 8 shillings

untrimmed beaver hat –
26 shillings and 8 pence

a cloak for the Earl of Leicester –
20 pounds

---

gown, knee-length for a young man, ankle-length for an older one. Alternatively a cloak may be worn outdoors. Although often highly decorative, the short cloak is not a particularly practical garment and needs constant readjustment. Hooded cloaks are excellent for winter and bad weather. Men with good legs wear tight hose, though these are very difficult to keep spotless on London's muddy streets. Those less favoured wear baggy breeches. Boys start wearing these when they are about seven but until then are dressed like girls. Thigh-length boots are another option for disguising slender calves.

### FEMALE FASHIONS

Women wear a flat-fronted bodice, stiffened by a busk of wood or whalebone.

X *Paul's Cross. A bishop occupies London's most famous pulpit. Note the presence (lower gallery) of the red-robed Lord Mayor with his sword-bearer. Choristers from the Cathedral are on the gallery roof. Attendance is almost entirely male. The sermon was a plea for funds to maintain the cathedral and ran to 51 pages when printed.*

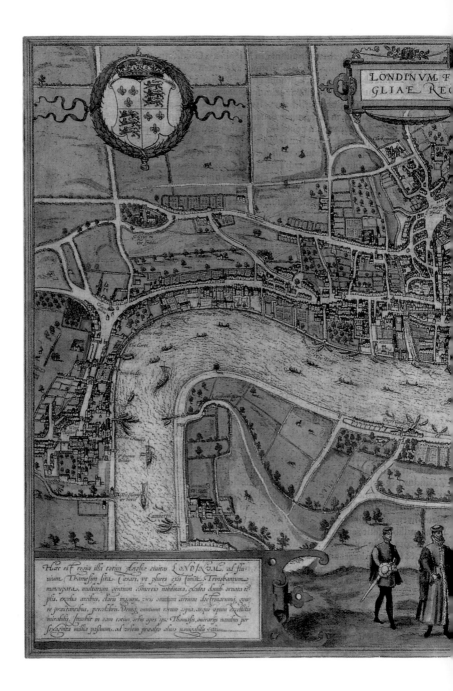

LONDINVM F
GLIAE REG

Hæc est Regia illa totius Angliæ ciuitas LONDINUM, ad flu-
uium Thamesim sita. Cæsari, ut plures exis timãt, Trinobantum
nuncupata, multarum gentium commercio nobilitata, multis domib, ornata ræ
plis, excelsis arcibus, clara ingeniis, ut in omnium animis doctrinarumq, genæ
re præstantibus, percelebris. Demü, omnium rerum copia, atque opum excellentia
mirabilis. Inuehit in eam totius orbis opes ipse Thamesis, quarariis nauibus per
sexaginta millia passuum, ad orbem præaltus aluco nauigabilis ﬂuuius.

XI *This map of London and Westminster by Frans Hogenberg and George Hoefnagel shows the metropolis around the time of the Queen's accession in 1558. The top panel describes London as 'most fruitful'. The river teems with traffic but its south bank is still largely rural.*

XII *Westminster, the focus of royal power. The confusion of buildings show how this area has been built piecemeal without an overall plan. When Parliament is in session Members assemble in the tall building in the centre of the picture. To the right looms Westminster Abbey, the church used for royal coronations.*

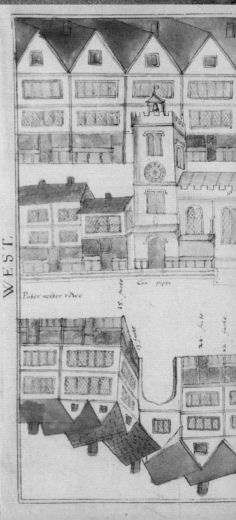

XIV  Cheapside, otherwise known as Westcheap, is lined with close-packed shops whose owners live on the floors above. The church is called St Michael-le-Quern, or St Michael at Corn because a corn market is held beside it. Notice the pipes bringing water to the Little Conduit at the rear of the church where water-carriers' vessels wait to be filled.

XV  *Nonsuch Palace at Cheam in Surrey was begun by Henry VIII but not completed until ten years after his death by the Earl of Arundel. It reverted to the Queen in 1592 and is used for hunting and entertaining.*
XVI  *Richmond Palace, upriver from London, was built in its present form by Henry VII, the Queen's grandfather, and is famous for its deer park. Note in the foreground the Morris dancers with their 'hobby horse' – the fashionable onlookers from the coach are giving a tip in appreciation.*

*Gloves are a perfect gift for the ladies, but they can also be filled with cash as a bribe. Clergy wear white gloves to show that they are 'clean' and not open to bribery.*

## GLOVES

Gloves are a fashion essential and an English speciality, richly embroidered, perfumed and even jewelled. The Queen herself possesses hundreds of pairs and regards them as a most acceptable gift, ideal for showing off her long, slender fingers. They are frequently carried, rather than worn.

Fans, made of feathers or leather, are another accessory that can be used to draw the eye to an elegant hand.

## RUFFS

The ruff is a large, round, pleated, detachable collar worn by both men and women, especially on formal occasions. They can look very good on some people in a portrait but they are uncomfortable to wear, expensive to buy and maintain and rarely flatter the wearer who has a short or fat neck. Yet practically every man or woman who can afford to wears one. Over the last 40 years they have got bigger and bigger, with some reaching 6 yards in length, 9 inches in depth and having 600 pleats. Starching and 'setting' a ruff can take hours, only for the

Over the skirt an apron will normally be worn. In the absence of pockets the girdle is used to attach one's scissors, penknife, seal, bodkin, ear-picker and pomander. Under the outer garments a linen smock is worn next to the skin but nothing else. The finest shoes are made of soft leather imported from Spain. The Queen's fantastically elaborate costumes require that she be pinned into them with hundreds of pins, as must all who dress in such high style.

*The women ... go dressed out in exceedingly fine clothes and give all their attention to their ruffs and stuffs, to such a degree, indeed, that ... many a one does not hesitate to wear velvet in the streets ... whilst at home they have not a piece of dry bread.*

FREDERICK, DUKE OF
WÜRTTEMBERG • 1592

result to be ruined in minutes by wind or rain. When going out for a special occasion it is therefore quite common for a person to have their ruff carried in a box by a servant and put on only upon arrival. Starching is best left to specialists, most of whom are Dutch women. Soft vegetable dyes are often used to colour the ruff ivory, pink, yellow or mauve, which looks better against the skin than stark, dead white. The Queen has, for some reason, taken against blue, which she has banned.

*Ruff stuff. Ralegh sporting the latest fashion – he is notoriously extravagant on clothes.*

### SOVEREIGN STYLE

Soon after her accession the Queen was introduced to silk stockings and swore she would never wear any others again. Each pair costs £2 – equal to the annual rent on a small farm. They are discarded at the end of a week and given to one of her ladies in waiting. In cold winters the Queen does revert to knitted woollen hose for warmth.

An inventory of the Queen's wardrobe, made in the 1590s, counted more than 3,000 items, including 102 'French gowns', 100 'loose gowns', 67 'round gowns', 99 robes, 127 cloaks, 85 doublets, 125 petticoats, 126 kirtles, 56 'saufegardes' (outer skirts) and 136 'foreparts' (stomachers).

In an attempt to interest Queen Elizabeth in the possibility of marrying him, Tsar Ivan the Terrible of Russia sent her two pieces of cloth of silver, four of cloth of gold, two gowns of white ermine, six lynx skins and 160 sable pelts.

In 1599 alone more than £700 was spent on 'fine linen for her Majesty's person'. Her annual clothing expenditure is reckoned in the region of £10,000. The Chancellor of the Exchequer has informed the House of Commons that her Majesty's apparel is 'royal and princely, beseeming her calling, but not sumptuous nor excessive'.

# IX · CELEBRATIONS

*Maundy Thursday · May Day · Midsummer
Bartholomew Fair · Charlton Horn Fair
Lord Mayor's Day · Accession Day · Marriage*

Londoners enjoy a variety of celebrations throughout the year, from Easter till the autumn. As a visitor, it is worth attending some of these events, if only to observe the manners and curious customs of the English. One of the high points of your stay might even be an invitation to a wedding.

## MAUNDY THURSDAY

MAUNDY THURSDAY COMES IMMEDIately before Good Friday. On this day the Queen goes to Westminster Abbey to repeat the ceremony of washing the feet of poor men and women who are chosen on account of their honesty and piety. Their number is equal to the years of the Queen's age. It is customary for Her Majesty to carry a large posy of sweet-smelling flowers and herbs in case the persons of the poor should smell rank.

The actual washing of the feet is carried out for the Queen by the Gentlemen of the Royal Laundry. After the foot-washing ceremony the Queen hands out to each poor person gifts of broadcloth, fish in token of Lent, and bread and a bowl of wine in token of the body and blood of Christ. They also receive a leather purse – green for women, white for men – with as many pennies as the Queen's age.

## MAY DAY

EVEN BEFORE IT IS LIGHT ON 1 MAY young people leave the city to go out into the country 'a-maying', to fetch fresh flowers, branches in blossom and hawthorn – 'may' – to decorate their houses and make into garlands. Girls wash their faces with May dew as a cure for freckles. The fairest maid is crowned 'Queen of the May'. The day is celebrated with games and sports, particularly archery. Maypoles are set up in the streets, most famously outside the church of St Andrew on Cornhill, whence it is known as St Andrew Undershaft, the maypole being higher even than the church's steeple. There is another great maypole in the Strand, outside Somerset House. As darkness falls bonfires are lit so that dancing and drinking can continue into the night.

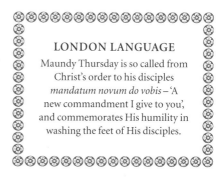

**LONDON LANGUAGE**

Maundy Thursday is so called from Christ's order to his disciples *mandatum novum do vobis* – 'A new commandment I give to you', and commemorates His humility in washing the feet of His disciples.

Plays are acted to tell the story of St George rescuing a maiden from a dragon. St George is England's patron saint and his day, 23 April, was once a great day of celebration. This ceased, however, by law, to be a holiday in the tenth year of the Queen's reign. But the story of St George is still much loved and so his remembrance has become a part of May Day. There are other plays that tell stories of Robin Hood and Maid Marion. Churchwardens pay for costumes of Robin and Marion and set the wearers to collecting cash for the parish funds.

> *The lords and ladies now*
> *abroad, for their disport*
> *and play,*
> *Do kiss sometimes upon*
> *the grass, and sometimes*
> *in the hay.*
>
> FRANCIS BEAUMONT AND
> JOHN FLETCHER • *THE KNIGHT*
> *OF THE BURNING PESTLE*

## LONDON LIVING

*All the young men and maids … run*
*gadding over night to the woods…*
*where they spend all the night … there*
*is a great Lord present amongst them, as*
*Superintendent and Lord over their*
*pastimes and sports, namely Satan,*
*prince of Hell … the chiefest jewel … is*
*their May-pole, which they bring home*
*with great veneration, then fall they to*
*dance about it, as the heathen people*
*did at the dedication of Idols, whereof*
*this is a perfect pattern … Of forty,*
*three score or a hundred maids going to*
*the wood overnight, there have scarcely*
*the third part of them returned*
*undefiled.*

PHILIP STUBBES
*THE ANATOMY OF ABUSES* • 1583

## MIDSUMMER

MIDSUMMER EVE IS CELEBRATED ON 23 June with the lighting of bonfires. It is held to be an auspicious time for divining the future, making love potions and watching for ghosts. Some believe that those who watch their church porch through the night will see the spirits of all the *living* people of that parish going in and those not seen coming out again will die before next Midsummer – as will those who keep the vigil but fall asleep. Certain flowers and herbs gathered on this night will give protection against evil spirits. The most powerful is St John's Wort, which is known in Latin as 'chase devil' and is used to exorcize haunted houses.

Midsummer Day, 24 June, was by old tradition the feast of St John the Baptist and marked by maypole dancing and archery contests in honour of Robin Hood. On this day the Sheriffs of London are elected. The Lord Mayor receives a red rose as the annual rent due for a footbridge between two houses in Seething Lane in the parish of All Hallows, Barking-by-the-Tower. These were once owned by the famous soldier Sir Robert Knollys, who defended London against the rebels led by Wat Tyler in 1381. In recognition of this service the red rose took the place

of the rent he formerly owed and is still paid to honour his memory.

*In towns and villages celebrations and dancing centre on the maypole – nobody seems to have arrived yet.*

## BARTHOLOMEW FAIR

IF YOU WOULD SEE FIRE-EATERS, FREAKS and fencing-masters, buy ballads or cure-all medicines or gimcrack jewelry, and run the gauntlet of a thousand scabby beggars, pickpockets and prostitutes, you cannot afford to miss Bartholomew Fair. You may see some of London's best actors, performing the parts for which they are famed, in booths set up for the occasion, and likewise strange beasts, dwarves, jugglers, and other curious sights not to be found elsewhere.

### LONDON LIVING

A quite recent custom, established in 1584, is the celebration of the sovereign's birthday, 7 September. Prayers of thanksgiving are said in each parish church. However many years Her Majesty has attained, that many of the oldest poor women of each parish pray for her long life and prosperous estate and are given spice cake, wine and 1, 2 or 3 pence, according to the means of the parish.

This ancient gathering dates from the reign of the first King Henry and takes place at Smithfield. It originally lasted for three days from the eve of St Bartholomew's Day, 24 August, but now stretches over two whole weeks. Although the profits were once intended for the benefit of the nearby priory and hospital of St Bartholomew the Great, the Corporation of the City now controls the fair. It was formerly the greatest place in all England for the sale of woollen cloth, in token of which it is opened by the Lord Mayor snipping a piece of the same. But now it has become more an occasion for bawdiness than for business.

## CHARLTON HORN FAIR

CHARLTON IS A VILLAGE TO THE SOUTH-east of London, beyond Greenwich. Tradition holds that King John was once hunting in the area and seduced the wife of a local miller, in compensation for which the king gave the miller the right to hold a fair on St Luke's Day, 18 October, that being the dedication of Charlton's parish church. Horns being the sign of a cuckold, this became called the Horn Fair, though this may, of course, really refer to St Luke, whose sign is an ox. Whatever the truth, many delight to come to the fair dressed in tawdry finery as kings or queens or as millers with horns on their heads.

There are scores of other fairs in the villages around London, from Stepney in the east to Pinner in the west. At Croydon there are two fairs; one, on 5 July, for cherries and another, on 2 October, for sheep and cattle. The fair at Peckham, to the south, lasts all the while from 21 July to 3 August. At Edmonton Fair, to the north, by old custom nothing of any practical use may be sold but gewgaws and gingerbread and such frippery.

## LORD MAYOR'S DAY

*Of these aldermen, one is elected every year … to be a magistrate named the mayor, who is in no less estimation with the Londoners, than the person of our most serene Lord, the Doge, is with us … and the day on which he enters upon his office, he is obliged to give a sumptuous entertainment to all the principal people in London, as well as to foreigners of distinction; … there must have been a thousand or more persons at table. This dinner lasted four hours or more.*

ANDREA TREVISANO

This was written a century ago. Nothing has changed in essentials except that everything is even bigger and more expensive. A new Lord Mayor of London is elected each year on 13 October, and on 29 October goes with the Aldermen in a great procession to Westminster Hall to take his oath of office before a judge of the Court of Exchequer. The Lord Mayor and his supporters travel most of the way along the river Thames in a magnificent barge, with oars decorated with silver and escorted by a fleet of barges belonging to the various livery companies. On his return the new Lord Mayor lands at St Paul's Wharf and rides in procession through the streets of the city with drummers and trumpeters, oboes and flutes, pikemen and standard-bearers and all the chief officers of the city – as the sword-bearer, Common Serjeant, Chamberlain, Common Crier, Sheriffs and Aldermen – wearing cap and gown and chains of silver or gold. All proceed to Guildhall, where they enjoy a splendid banquet.

## ACCESSION DAY

Domino factum est istud et est mirabile in oculis nostris – *This is the Lord's doing and it is marvellous in our eyes.*

ELIZABETH I ON HEARING OF HER ACCESSION

*Preceded by his sword-bearer, the Lord Mayor rides in procession to take up his office.*

The accession of the Queen has been celebrated on 17 November every year since 1568, the tenth anniversary of her coming to the throne. It was added to the list of holy days in 1576 but it is not a day of rest. Bells are rung, the guns of the Tower of London are fired off in salute, special prayers are said for the sovereign's life and health and there are bonfires and fireworks at night.

## MARRIAGE

WHILE YOU MAY HAVE NO PLANS TO get married in London yourself, you are more or less bound to see a wedding and, if you make friends with a local family, are quite likely to be invited to one. So it may be helpful, as well as interesting, to know a little about just how things are usually done.

## SETTING THE DAY

Setting a suitable day is by no means straightforward. You may not marry in Lent. Or during Rogationtide. Or Trinity. Or Advent. Unless, of course, you can pay for a special licence of dispensation to do so. There are also another 144 days on which you may *not* get married. There is no scriptural basis for this whatsoever, but it is custom and zealously enforced by the Church of England. The common folk say, 'marry in Lent, you'll surely repent'.

In the countryside marriages are most common when there is least work to be done and most produce to be eaten. In London these are not great considerations and so weddings take place there throughout the year. Despite often miserable weather, both February and November are popular months, especially with those marrying for a second or third time. They care far less for the frolics of the young. And there are few other festivities or distractions so a large attendance may be relied on.

## THE BANNS

The wedding must be proclaimed at least three weeks in advance by the calling of 'banns' in the church of the parish where it is to take place. This is to enable objections to be raised on any of the following grounds:
(a) One of the couple is already married or contracted to another, the latter being more common than the former.

(b) The intended partners are too young; the groom must be at least 14, the bride 12. Either case would be most unusual. In practice both are normally double those respective ages.
(c) If under 21, either have not the consent of their parents.
(d) The intended couple are too closely related by blood or marriage. The Church of England recognizes 30 such forbidden couplings, a printed notice of which shall be found displayed prominently in every parish church. Marriage between cousins is permitted.

## THE CHURCH

*As marriage is a civil contract, it must be done so in public, as that it may have the testimony of men. As marriage is a religious contract, it must be so done as it may have the benediction of the priest.*

JOHN DONNE

### LONDON LIVING

One last custom must be noted. When the bride and groom go to their bed any young unmarried men and women go with them to their chamber. There they sit at the bed's end, facing away from the bridal pair, who pass them their stockings, the bride's to the men, the groom's to the maidens. Then each throw them backwards over their head and the first that hits either the bride or groom on the nose will be the next to be married – or so they say.

## LONDON LIVING

Although some Puritans hold it popish, every normal wedding involves the giving of a ring. Contrary to old custom, however, the priest now neither blesses the ring nor sprinkles it with holy water. Nor is it to be placed on each finger in succession, as was once customary.

The ring is placed on the fourth finger of the left hand of the bride from whence a vein connects direct with the heart itself, as a token of love. The bride alone takes a ring, though no one can say why the groom does not.

### THE CELEBRATIONS

*After the banquet and feast there beginneth a vain, mad and unmannerly fashion. For the bride must be brought into an open dancing place ... then there is such a lifting up and discovering of the damsel's clothes and of other women's apparel, that a man might think all the dancers had cast all shame behind them ... Then must the poor bride keep foot with all dancers and refuse none, how scabbed, foul, drunken, rude and shameless soever he be.*

MILES COVERDALE
THE CHRISTIAN STATE OF MATRIMONY • 1552

In the days of our grandfathers the wedding ceremony took place most often at the church porch. Now it must be inside the church, between the hours of 8 o'clock in the morning and noon, in front of a congregation. The ceremony must be conducted according to the prescribed words of the *Book of Common Prayer*. After the ceremony the wedding must be written in the register of the parish, to stand as a record of it. Unless all these things are done thus, 'it is but regulated adultery; it is not marriage'.

The bride is 'given up' by her father or some other man of her household, to signify his assent. Master Hooker also charges that 'It putteth women in mind of a duty whereunto the very imbecility of their nature and sex doth bind them,

namely, to be always directed, guided and ordered by others.'

After the church ceremonies the celebrations begin. To see the most lively kind you should go to some nearby country village, like Leyton or Hackney, Ealing or Bermondsey. The bride goes to and from church with music, dancing the morris. Young men tilt at the quintain for a garland – or a kiss. The wedding feast normally includes beef and mustard, mince pies and a custard, spiced wine and huge quantities of beer. Guests receive gifts of ribbons and laces, embroidered gloves and garters of blue (a lingering echo of bridal reverence for the Virgin Mary). Everyone is welcome, though as a guest you should bring wine or a cheese or a pudding or some great fish to add to the fare.

# X · ENTERTAINMENT

*Pleasure Districts · The Theatre*
*Music · Sport*

Londoners are as serious about enjoying themselves as they are about making money. And providing pleasure to others can make you seriously rich, as the career of Mr Alleyn so clearly shows. So whether it's sport, singing or the stage, whatever your particular pastime, it can probably be found within – or, more likely, just outside – the walls of London town.

## PLEASURE DISTRICTS

The city of London, within the boundaries defined by law, is closely governed by the Lord Mayor and Aldermen, who are no friends to play or idleness. If you are seeking diversion you must, therefore, look elsewhere.

The pleasure ground known as Spring Gardens adjoins the royal park of St James's Palace by Charing Cross. The location makes this a resort of the fashionable. You will find butts for archery and a bathing pond, but mostly the well-dressed and well-spoken come here to stroll on well-kept turf amid shady trees, and preen to be in such company in such a setting. The same may be said of Moorfields, on the north side of the city walls, where trees are being planted and gravel walks laid

out for sober citizens and their wives to take the evening air. Members of some City Companies may resort to the private gardens around their Livery Halls. To the east of the city, the mean riverside districts of Wapping

⊛⊛⊛⊛⊛⊛⊛⊛⊛⊛⊛⊛⊛⊛⊛

### LONDON LANGUAGE

*arquebus* – also harquebus, long-barrelled gun supported on a forked rest
*cittern* – musical instrument similar to a guitar
*coney-catcher* – confidence trickster
*hautboy* – oboe
*madrigal* – repetitive composition for more than one voice but with no fixed form
*pippin* – apple grown from seed
*poniard* – a dagger for stabbing, rather than slashing, from the Latin *pugnus* meaning fist
*popinjay* – gaudy, bird-shaped target, hence also a conceited, overly fashionable man
*round* – musical composition for two or more voices, each of which sings the same melody but starts at a different time
*tabor* – small drum, usually used to accompany a fife
*virginal* – boxed, legless keyboard stringed instrument
*zany* – a clown, from the Venetian for John Giovanni

⊛⊛⊛⊛⊛⊛⊛⊛⊛⊛⊛⊛⊛⊛⊛

and Shadwell abound with low places for drinking, gaming, bowling and cock fights, and are chiefly the resort of seamen, strumpets and scoundrels. You know whether or not you belong there.

The largest area given over to amusement is the Bankside, in Southwark, at the southern end of London Bridge. There you will find the main theatres, as well as the baiting of bears and bulls, dozens of taverns and the city's most notorious bawdy-houses. Many come to this area by boat and land at a place called Paris Garden, so called from the ancient manor house of Robert de Paris and now well known for gaming and tippling. By night do keep to the paths in this thickly wooded locality unless in a group.

*This recent sketch of the Swan Theatre by a Dutch visitor shows the proximity of the actors to the audience.*

## THE THEATRE

*Will not a filthy play, with the blast of a trumpet, sooner call thither a thousand, than an hour's tolling of a bell bring to the sermon a hundred? … Whereas if you resort to the Theatre, the Curtain and other places of plays in the city, you shall on the Lord's day have those places … so full as… they can throng …*

JOHN STOCKWOOD
*A SERMON PREACHED AT PAUL'S CROSS* • 1578

You can still come across plays being put on in the courtyards of inns, where it was long the custom to perform, such as the Bull in Bishopsgate or the Cross Keys in Gracechurch Street; but actors now much prefer to present themselves in a theatre. This enables them to make a charge for entrance, rather than hope a crowd will be generous before it drifts off. It also does away with the distracting noises made by potboys, maids and ostlers in an inn, and by street-sellers, ballad-singers and the general bustle of traffic outside it. Thanks to this change alone actors no longer have to make constant recourse to jigs and foolery and mock-fights to attract the attention of an audience but, commanding them from a stage, can use their voices – and the finest words – to full effect.

Having a permanent home also enables a company of actors to build up a much bigger store of costumes, armour, playbooks, musical instruments and so on, than if all these have to be kept and carried from place to place in a handcart.

The Rose Theatre, for example, possesses such items for stage effect as:

A flight of steps, two steeples, a beacon, a bay tree, two mossy banks, a tree of golden apples and a rainbow.

A snake, a dragon, two coffins, a cauldron and an assortment of 'dead limbs'.

Items such as the blood, heart, liver and lungs of a sheep, used to simulate disembowelment on stage, must, of course, be purchased fresh for every performance.

London's first theatres – the Theatre and the Curtain – were put up on the northeast side of the city, at Shoreditch, in the former grounds of Holywell Priory. They were thus within a short and easy walk of the City – but outside its jurisdiction. Here Shakespeare presented for the first time his *Romeo and Juliet, The Taming of the Shrew* and *Henry V.* When the ground lease ran out the company took the Theatre down and used its timbers to build the Globe, on Bankside. The Curtain remains. On Bankside the rivals to the Globe are the Rose and the Swan. Burbage and Shakespeare's rivals, Henslowe and Alleyn, are building a new venture, the Fortune, on the opposite side of the city, just outside the northern wall, near Cripplegate.

*Our players are not as the players beyond sea, a sort of squirting bawdy comedians, that have whores and common courtesans to play women's parts, and forbear no immodest speech or unchaste action that may procure laughter ... but our representations honourable and full of gallant resolution, not consisting, like theirs, of a pantaloon, a whore and a zany, but of emperors, kings and princes, whose true tragedies they do vaunt.*

THOMAS NASHE • *PIERCE PENNILESS* • 1592

Plays are presented in the afternoon, at around 2 o'clock. If you want to know what piece is being offered and who is in it, look out for the printed handbills distributed beforehand. Trumpeters and the flying of a flag indicate the actual starting of a performance. Thanks to Puritan pressure, plays may no longer be staged on a Sunday or in Lent. Plague outbreaks likewise shut down the playhouses for months at a time. When this happens the actors go on tour, even as far as Germany. Successive Lord Mayors have made it clear that they would gladly close down playhouses and playing permanently if they could, but the Privy Council refuses, knowing that 'Her Majesty sometimes took delight in these pastimes', and the actors therefore must practise before less exalted eyes.

At the theatre you pay one penny to stand in the area around the stage as a 'groundling'. To go under cover costs another penny, a stool to sit at your ease one penny more and a cushion yet another. All together as many as 2,000 or 3,000 of you may crowd into the arena, yielding an average taking for the proprietors of £8, rather more than the £6 a writer would expect to receive for the script of a new play. You'll get your money's worth, since before and after the actual plays the actors may also sing, dance, juggle or tumble. You can buy tobacco by the pipeful at 3 pence, also ale, wine, pies, pasties, oranges and pippin apples.

Audiences usually contain more men than women, thanks to the numbers of gentleman students from the Inns of Court and apprentices stealing time whenever their masters are away on business. But all ranks of persons may be seen, from carter to courtier. Only the Puritans are absent – because they choose to be.

### YOU CANNOT BELIEVE IT!

*The player, when he cometh in, must ever begin with telling where he is … Now ye shall have three ladies walk to gather flowers, and then we must believe the stage to be a garden. By and by we hear news of shipwreck in the same place, and then we are to blame, if we accept it not for a rock … While in the meantime two armies fly in, represented with four swords and bucklers, and then what hard heart will not receive it for a pitched field? … of time … ordinary it is that two … fall in love. After many traverses, she is got with child, delivered of a fair boy, he … groweth a man, falls in love, and is ready to get another child; and all this in two hours space.*

SIR PHILIP SIDNEY
*AN APOLOGIE FOR POETRIE* • 1595

If you only ever go to see one play, make it *The Spanish Tragedy* by the late Thomas Kyd, by far the most popular play ever performed in London's theatres.

Horatio, son of Hieronimo, marshal of Spain, is hanged in a garden after a tryst by night with Bel-imperia, daughter of the Duke of Castile.

Horatio's murderers are Bel-imperia's brother, Lorenzo, and Horatio's rival, Balthazar.

*A climactic moment in Kyd's ever-popular* The Spanish Tragedy.

After recovering from a mad rage of grief, Hieronimo revenges himself by staging a play before them.

In the course of this Lorenzo and Balthazar are murdered and Bel-imperia stabs herself.

Hieronimo then bites out his own tongue and kills himself.

*The Spanish Tragedy* has been revived and revised many times, but never fails to draw huge audiences. Regular playgoers have noted a certain similarity of plot with Shakespeare's *The Tragical History of Hamlet, Prince of Denmark.*

*The English pass their time learning at the play what is happening abroad.*

THOMAS PLATTER • 1599

### HOW DOES HE DO IT?

Of all the many current quill-drivers, William Shakespeare seems to achieve the most consistent success with London audiences, whether writing history, tragedy or comedy. (Although he does seem oddly keen on setting his plays in Italy. He might just as well say 'foreign'. No matter.) Mr S. already has some 20 works to his credit; but one will have to suffice as an exemplar of his remarkable talents.

*Henry V* can scarcely claim to be original subject-matter. A hack piece called *The Famous Victories of Henry the Fifth* has been around now for the best part of 20 years. But Shakespeare's reworking of it has (risking the pun) taken the stage by storm. Scarcely surprising you might say — boyish but plucky English king and hopelessly outnumbered army of bare-arsed archers completely rout an overwhelming French force of arrogant armoured aristocrats at Agincourt. Fairly certain to please the crowd? Well, yes – but it's how he tells it.

At the beginning the king is in council. The historical scene-setting – why Henry can rightfully claim the French throne – is got through without making the audience feel as ignorant as the king's councillors are shown to be. At the end the victorious monarch is shown up like a tongue-tied schoolboy wooing the French princess in such mangled French that he transforms himself from an object of fear into one almost of ridicule. The English-speaking audience laughs at him – and at themselves, knowing they could do no better. Having shared in the exultation of his victory, they share in his humiliation and go out uplifted but also smiling in sympathy.

In between there is a constant counterpoint between great events and petty characters, the serious, the sad, the silly and the sublime. And all this, as the Chorus reminds us, accomplished with 'four or five rusty foils' as the 'vasty fields of France' are conjured and compressed within 'the Wooden O'.

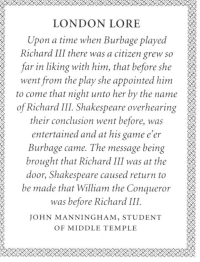

### LONDON LORE

*Upon a time when Burbage played Richard III there was a citizen grew so far in liking with him, that before she went from the play she appointed him to come that night unto her by the name of Richard III. Shakespeare overhearing their conclusion went before, was entertained and at his game e'er Burbage came. The message being brought that Richard III was at the door, Shakespeare caused return to be made that William the Conqueror was before Richard III.*

JOHN MANNINGHAM, STUDENT OF MIDDLE TEMPLE

*MUSIC*

---

*Supper being ended and the Music books, according to the custom, being brought to the table: the mistress of the house presented me with a part, earnestly requesting me to sing. But when after many excuses I protested that I could not: every one began to wonder. Yea, some whispered to others, demanding how I was brought up.*

THOMAS MORLEY • *PLAIN AND EASY INTRODUCTION TO PRACTICAL MUSIC* • 1597

*The Queen herself plays daily and expertly on the virginals.*

If you are staying in a private household you can count on being called to join in the singing at some point. Any gentleman or lady should know how to take part in the singing of a madrigal, even if their voice is not fine enough to carry off a solo. The English love music and have much reason to rejoice in their own achievements. English music teachers are in demand as far away as Italy. Henry VIII himself played the lute and composed several songs. The Queen plays expertly on the virginals. Musicians playing trumpets and flutes accompany her when she sails in her royal barge on the Thames. Even barbers' shops usually have a lute available for waiting customers to while away the time with. William Bathe boasts in his *Brief Introduction to the Skill of Song* that in a single month he taught a boy of eight 'to sing at the first sight, to be so indifferent for all parts, alterations, cleves, flats and sharps, that he could sing a part of that kind, of which he never learned any song'.

*First, it is a knowledge easily taught and quickly learned ...*

*2. The exercise of singing is delightful to Nature and good to preserve the health of Man.*

*3. It doth strengthen all parts of the breast and doth open the pipes.*

*4. It is a singular good remedy for stuttering and stammering in the speech.*

*5. It is the best means to procure a perfect pronunciation and to make a good orator.*

WILLIAM BYRD • *PSALMS, SONNETS AND SONGS OF SADNESS AND PIETIE* • 1588

## DANCING

In polite circles you will be expected to dance and, if you are French or Italian, to do so very well. The Queen herself was, when younger, an excellent and enthusiastic dancer and still loves to watch others dance. According to the French ambassador 'when her Maids dance she follows the cadence with her head, hand and foot. She rebukes them if they do not dance to her liking and without doubt she is mistress of the art, having learnt in the Italian manner.'

*Dancing does not require equal numbers of males and females to take part.*

Court dances are stately. The grave *pavane* may be danced even by those well past youth, wearing long gowns and even hats and gloves. The *allemande* is another processional dance, but in three parts. When the music stops, dancers converse with their partners; each time it starts again it is faster, ending gaily. This is the sort of dance in which the feet never leave the floor and hence is known as a *dance basse.*

The *galliard, cinquepace* and *coranto* are much more lively. The most spectacular is the *volta,* where the gentleman clasps the lady round the waist and lifts her right off the ground, spinning as he does so. For this dance it is advisable to take off one's sword and cloak to avoid tripping over them. Dances involving running, leaping or lifting are called *haute dance.*

Country dances, to the simple music of pipe and tabor, are also on occasion seen at Court. In taverns and in London streets and on suburban village greens at holidays, the dances of the common people are joyous jigs and rounds, accompanied among the young by much flirtation and kissing.

## SPORT

### BAITING OF BEARS AND BULLS

The baiting of bears and bulls at Bankside has been going on for at least half a century. The extinction of bears in England means that they must be imported, which is expensive. They are therefore

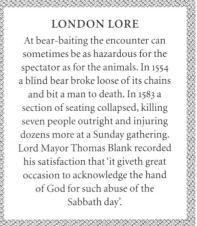

### LONDON LORE

At bear-baiting the encounter can sometimes be as hazardous for the spectator as for the animals. In 1554 a blind bear broke loose of its chains and bit a man to death. In 1583 a section of seating collapsed, killing seven people outright and injuring dozens more at a Sunday gathering. Lord Mayor Thomas Blank recorded his satisfaction that 'it giveth great occasion to acknowledge the hand of God for such abuse of the Sabbath day'.

rarely killed outright until they have had several encounters to let the bear-master recoup his outlay, unless for a royal entertainment. Besides, once the bear is dead, his carcass is useless except to be fed to the dogs that killed him. A bull is much cheaper and, once dead, can be sold for butcher's meat, the more so since Londoners generally believe that its torments sweeten the flesh for eating.

*Bulls or bears? Rival attractions at Bankside. Note the rows of mastiffs straining at the leash in their kennels.*

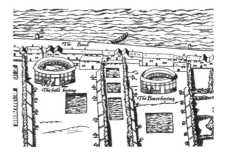

The standard procedure is to rope a bull to a stake, giving it a ring about 30 ft across to move in. Mastiffs, specially bred for the task, are set on and bets laid on their performance. To defend itself, the bull aims not to gore the dogs but to toss them 'so high in the air that he may break his neck in the fall'. Look out for the skill of dog-handlers using long sticks to break the dog's fall.

Baiting of bears and bulls takes place in the theatres and, in the main holiday periods, pays the promoter about twice what a play brings in.

*A knife is offered to Her Majesty to deliver the* coup de grâce *at the hunt.*

---

### COCK-FIGHTING

*In the city of London ... cock-fights are held ... and I saw the place which is built like a theatre. In the centre on the floor stands a circular table ... where the cocks are teased and incited to fly at one another, while those with wagers ... sit closest around the circular disc, but the Spectators who are merely present on their entrance penny sit around higher up, watching with eager pleasure the fierce and angry fight between the cocks as these wound each other to death with spurs and beaks.*

THOMAS PLATTER • *TRAVELS IN ENGLAND* • 1599

Cocks that refuse to fight or try to flee the ring have their necks wrung on the spot. Cocks that survive a lethal encounter, no matter if badly injured, are rewarded for their courage and kept to breed from and may be sold for a high price. There is a permanent cock-pit at Whitehall Palace, but cock-fights may be easily organized in the court-yard of any large inn.

There is another holiday sport called 'throwing at cocks', in which people throw sticks and stones at a tethered cock from 40 or 50 paces. Whoever gives it the death-blow can take it home to eat. Another version involves throwing a stick or stone hard and accurately enough to stun the bird or knock it over long enough for the thrower to grab it by the feet, then break its neck. You are certain to see this on a Shrove Tuesday when it is a traditional part of the celebrations before the onset of Lent.

---

### HUNTING AND HAWKING

*I think it not amiss to ... give that recreation precedency of place, which in mine opinion doth many degrees go before and precede all other, as being most royal for the stateliness thereof, most artificial for the wisdom and cunning thereof, and most manly and warlike for the use and endurance thereof. And this I hold to be the hunting of wild beasts ... the stag, the buck, the roe, the hare, the fox, the badger, the otter, the boar, the goat and suchlike.*

GERVASE MARKHAM
*COUNTRY CONTENTMENTS*

The English call hunting the sport of kings. At the eastern end of Whitehall Palace, the Royal Mews houses the Queen's hawks and their handlers. The walled parks around the royal palaces at St James's, Greenwich and Richmond were all created as hunting enclosures, and are stocked with deer and hares, where the monarch and favoured courtiers can take daily exercise. At greater distance from London but still within the day's ride are hunting grounds around the palaces of Theobald's in Hertfordshire and Nonsuch and Hampton Court in Surrey (see Chapter XI). At Enfield, to the north of London, the 'Great Standing' was built, four storeys high, so that when the Queen's late father could no longer follow the chase on horseback he could still watch its progress.

According to Stow, Londoners would hunt much more often than they do if only they had the time and the opportunity. Some, of course, take the risk of going into the countryside round about the capital to poach game with nets and snares, slingshots and crossbows. For this reason it is illegal to own a crossbow unless the owner is also worth £100 a year, which should mean that he would be above such knavery, though some delight in poaching their neighbour's game for sheer devilment.

Poaching on privately owned land is punishable by death if committed at night, or if the poacher disguises himself or obscures his face to avoid being identified. If poaching is done in daytime, without a disguise, it is a felony punishable by a fine or imprisonment.

## LONDON LORE

It is customary each year for the Lord Mayor and Aldermen to ride out to inspect the conduits which bring water into the city. This excursion is accompanied by a banquet, after which they hunt for hares and foxes in the fields to the west of St Giles church. This area is hence known as 'SoHo' – which is the cry given by the master of the hunt to signal 'The prey is seen!'

### COURSING

Coursing is the sport of hunting game by sight not scent, usually, but not exclusively, with greyhounds. Originally this was a practical pursuit to put something in the pot, but it has become a competitive event since the Queen ordered Thomas, Duke of Norfolk, Earl Marshal of England, to draw up a code of rules, known as the Laws of the Leash. These rules are now accepted by all the nobility and used to govern pursuits organized in their private parks.

## FENCING

In the present century the ancient knightly broadsword has been replaced by the rapier, an altogether deadlier and more demanding weapon. Instead of carrying a small buckler for defence, the swordsman carries a poniard dagger to block his opponent's blows and to use as a secondary weapon. In the swordfight strength now counts far less than skill, and this must be acquired through instruction and long practice. In 1537, when Italian masters seemed set to dominate the fencing schools of the capital, King Henry VIII granted a charter to The Company of the Masters of Defence of London, recognizing them officially as a guild of instructors.

Members of the guild charge fees for their teaching but also earn money from public displays, known as prizes, which additionally give them the opportunity to attract new pupils. Prizes usually begin with a procession, accompanied by drummers, to attract an audience. Normally the contestants and the organizers, who will act as judges, gather at Blackfriars, where there are several rival fencing schools, then proceed via Ludgate Hill into the city proper. The actual contests take place in the yard of an inn. The innkeeper may make a fixed admission charge, or accept a share of the takings or content himself with the profit from selling drink to the crowd. The fights may last as long as a play at the theatre, because there will normally be four fencers taking part, each fighting two bouts with each of three different weapons, making 24 passes to decide the overall victor.

*George Silver, having the perfect knowledge of all manner of weapons and being experienced in all manner of fights ... admonish the noble, ancient, victorious, valiant and most brave nation of Englishmen to take heed how they submit themselves into the hands of Italian teachers of Defence.*

GEORGE SILVER • *PARADOXES OF DEFENCE* • 1599

## THE QUINTAIN

The quintain was formerly used to train knights in the use of the lance but is now commonly an amusement for holidays. It consists of a revolving dummy on a post that is fixed in the ground, its arms outstretched, one with a shield, which is the mark, the other with a heavy bag of sand. According to Stow this exercise is particularly popular at Christmas:

*I have seen a Quintain set up on Cornhill, by the Leaden Hall ... and made great pastime; for he that hit not the broad end of the Quintain, was of all men laughed to scorn, and he that hit it full, if he rode not the faster, had a sound blow in his neck ... I have also in the summer season seen some upon the river of Thames rowed in wherries, with staves in their hands, flat at the fore end, running against one another, and, for the most part, one or both overthrown, and well ducked.*

If you want to understand the game, you really have to go and watch with an experienced player. There are courts at the royal palaces of Whitehall, Greenwich and Hampton Court.

## TENNIS

It is said that every Frenchman is born with a racket in his hand and that even among the poor in France there are as many tennis players as there are ale-drinkers in England. King Henry VIII was a keen player of this game and it has remained very popular among all the nobility. Because tennis requires an indoor court, which is expensive to build, it has remained a sport for the privileged few.

England has taken up the game from France where play begins with the call 'Tenez' – hence the English name of the game, tennis. Players require wooden rackets which are shaped like paddles and are strung with sheep's intestines. The ball they play with is stuffed with human hair and soon goes out of shape, making it good for only one game. Players hit the ball to each other across a net and off the roof of a sort of shed, called a penthouse, which runs round three sides of the court. The rules and the scoring system are so complicated that it would take pages to explain them.

*A bowl-alley is the place where there are three things thrown away besides bowls, to wit, time, money and curses … The best sport in it is … he enjoys it that looks on and bets not.*

JOHN EARLE
*MICROCOSMOGRAPHIE*

## BOWLS

Bowling has been played, both by men and women, for as long as anyone can remember. There are different versions of the game in different parts of the country, but usually there are nine pins set in a diamond shape and each player bowls three bowls to knock down as many as possible, the fallen pins being set up between the bowling of each one. Hence the game is also known as 'ninepins'.

Bets, but usually only small sums, may be laid on the contest or the loser may agree to buy ale for the winner.

### LONDON LORE

As every London schoolboy knows, in 1588 Sir Francis Drake was playing bowls on Plymouth Hoe when he heard the Spanish Armada had been sighted, and famously said, 'There is plenty of time to win this game and thrash the Spaniards, too'. Actually the tide was too low at the time for the English fleet to put to sea so Drake chose, by playing out his game, to assure his captains of his confidence in victory.

A new form of the ancient game of bowling has been spreading in the present century. In this form a jack ball is used as a movable target and the bowler uses a ball weighted with a bias to one side, so that it follows a curving path, demanding much greater skill of the bowler. Men of the highest rank play this form of bowling and there are greens at both Whitehall Palace and Hampton Court. The older, rather than the younger, especially favour bowling because it requires patience and cunning, rather than speed or strength.

## ARCHERY

*Exercises in the long bow by citizens … [are] now almost clean left off and forsaken … our archers for want of room to shoot abroad creep into bowling alleys and ordinary dicing houses.*

JOHN STOW • *A SURVAY OF LONDON* • 1598

If you are taken to watch archery practice and feel the urge to join in – don't. It's a great deal more difficult than it looks and takes a training starting from childhood to develop the necessary muscles and the skill of estimating the effect of the breeze. By his mid-20s a man should be capable of hitting a target a furlong – 220 yards – distant.

The longbow is no longer the war-winning weapon of yesteryear but the skilled archer is still held in high esteem. King Henry VIII in his youth was a fine archer and granted Master Roger Ascham a pension of £10 a year

for writing his treatise on archery, *Toxophilus, the School of Shooting*. This was the first learned defence of the idea that physical training was an essential part of an education.

English law obliges each of the Queen's male subjects that are aged between seven and sixty (except priests and judges) to possess a bow equal to his own height and arrows of appropriate length. The best bows are made of yew, cheap ones of elm. Regular practice, however, is nowadays often neglected, especially in London, where fields in which once a man might safely shoot are being built over every day.

The main practice area for those who still are keen archers is Finsbury Fields, outside the city wall to the north, where some 150 targets of different kinds stand at various lengths, from 180 to 380 yards, so that the archer can learn to judge distances. Rather than being numbered, the targets have names, such as Walker's Drag, Baines' Noodle, Queen's Stake and Maidenblush. Mile End Waste, a mile to the east of the Tower of London, has another archery field. When a bowman is about to shoot he shouts out 'Fast!' as a warning. If you ever hear this – stand still!

The longbow is still used in hunting – more especially in poaching – being virtually silent. For the same reason the crossbow, often modified to fire small balls of lead or clay, is still widely used to shoot birds out of a tree, or small game such as hares. The bird falls without a cry and the hunter may then shoot another of the flock, whereas the sound of a gun would scare them all away.

## WRESTLING

*Each striveth how to take hold of the other with his best advantage, and to bear his adverse party down; wherein whosoever overthroweth his mate, in such sort as that either his back, or the one shoulder and contrary heel do touch the ground, is accounted to give the fall.*

R. CAREW • *SURVEY OF CORNWALL*

Wrestling is popular among the poor but was also much enjoyed by King Henry VIII, both to watch and to take part in himself. In England there are very distinct styles of wrestling in different regions of the country. Thus there is one style in the remote northern counties of Cumberland and Westmorland, another in neighbouring Lancashire and yet another in Devon and Cornwall in the far southwest. As men from all counties come to London, you are quite likely to see any of these styles there. Wrestling matches are a special feature of the celebration of Lammas-tide, which is the first day of August.

## FOOTBALL

*Unknown malefactors to the number of over one hundred assembled themselves unlawfully and played a certain unlawful game called football, by means of which there was amongst them a great affray, likely to result in homicides and serious accident.*

QUARTER SESSIONS RECORDS OF *THE COUNTY OF MIDDLESEX* • 1576

Football requires a ball and very little else. There are almost no rules. The game is usually played between neighbouring villages, each of whose men try to get the ball from a starting-point between the two back into their home territory. In the capital, contests are usually between the apprentices of London and those of Westminster. Tripping, kicking and punching opponents all appear to be part of what often seems to the onlooker like a common affray. The authorities frown on football, which has been repeatedly banned by the monarch, the Lord Mayor and the magistrates, as a threat to public order, a cause of needless injury to Her Majesty's subjects and a distraction from archery practice. The English seem, however, to be addicted to this pastime and disobey all commands to desist from it.

# XI · AWAYDAYS

*Pleasant Places · Eastward Ho! · Other Directions*
*London's Lifelines · Great Houses*

MANY LONDONERS ARE COMING TO believe that, as London gets ever bigger, noisier and more bewildering, the only way to live there is to get away from it occasionally. It therefore seems appropriate to conclude with suggestions for a number of diverting excursions into the suburbs and countryside around the capital.

## PLEASANT PLACES

*The manner of the most gentlemen and noble men is to house themselves (if possibly they may) in the suburbs of the city, because most commonly the air there being somewhat at large, the place is healthy, and through the distance from the body of the town, the noise not much, and so consequently quiet ... Also for commodity we find many lodgings both spacious and roomy, with gardens and orchards very delectable.*

CIVIL AND UNCIVIL LIFE · 1576

All remark on the continuing expansion of the city into the surrounding countryside.

Stow recalls the eastern side of the city as it was in his childhood, when just outside the walls a boy could still pick berries from the hedges and buy milk warm from the cow. He expresses disgust at what has become of Mile End – 'this common field, being sometime the beauty of this city on that part is so encroached upon by building of filthy cottages ... inclosures and laystalls, that in some places scarce remaineth a sufficient highway for the meeting of carriages and droves of cattle'.

## EASTWARD HO!

THE IMMEDIATE RIVERSIDE AREAS downstream have little to recommend them, but only a mile or two to their north the outlying settlements are still pleasant places for you to walk to and through. The building of almshouses alongside the roads running eastwards out of the city confirms the desirability of this locality for either residence or retirement.

Shoreditch, the first home of London's theatres, is still home to many actors and writers who worship and are buried at the parish church of St Leonard. Whitechapel to the east is noted for London's bell-foundry. At Bethnal Green is Kirby's Castle, a fair mansion built by the city merchant Sir John Kirby. To the south, opposite the Saxon parish church of St Dunstan's, Stepney, is Great Place, the former home of Lord Mayor Sir Henry Colet, then, briefly, of Thomas Cromwell before his disgrace. From here a paved road runs all the way to Bow Bridge over the river Lea, much favoured by anglers, and the boundary between the counties of Middlesex and Essex. The Lea, tidal upstream as far as Old Ford, has banks lined with watermills grinding grain from Hertfordshire and Essex for the ovens of the bakers of Stratford. Makers of baskets and matting still come here to gather osiers and reeds for their craft, but some Dutchmen have established a dye-works to make red cloth, so other industries may soon invade this delightful spot. In the meantime the goodwives of Bromley-by-Bow are pleased to sell you home-baked eel pies or cherries and cream. Further to the east, past Stratford, Romford has a great cattle market and, on the river, at Barking, the main fishing port of London, you can view the ruins of England's second largest nunnery.

## OTHER DIRECTIONS

CLERKENWELL, NORTH OF THE CITY walls and watered by the river Fleet, was once a religious precinct with a nunnery, the priory of the Knights Hospitaller and the monastery of the Charterhouse. The nunnery's vineyard has long gone, its church taken over for the parish. Charterhouse has been converted into a residence in the Queen's gift. Most of St John's Priory was torn down for its materials but the gateway

**LONDON LANGUAGE**

*commodity* – convenience
*dole* – free allowance, usually of bread
*laystall* – a dung-heap or midden
*Master of the Revels* – organizer of royal entertainments and official censor
*quartan* – recurring every four days
*stews* – brothels

survives as the office of the Master of the Revels, Edmund Tilney, whose approval must be sought before the presentation of any play upon the stage. Anyone anxious to see Shakespeare or Jonson or Dekker or Nashe in person might, therefore, find it well worthwhile to haunt its vicinity. Great families of name – Cavendishes, Berekeleys and Chaloners – have mansions here, but Turnmill Street is scandalous for stews and thieves' kitchens.

Beyond Clerkenwell, at Islington, you can idle away an afternoon shooting duck and spooning down the local speciality, spiced custard. At dark, however, avoid the place as the warmth of the brick ovens there draws many who would as soon cut a throat as a purse. John Norden, the Queen's own mapmaker, notes the same of the area around the ancient church at St Pancras to the west of Islington:

'Although this place be as it were forsaken of all, and true men seldom frequent the same but upon divine occasions, yet is it visited and usually haunted of Rogues, vagabonds, harlots and thieves, who assemble not there to pray, but to wait for prey, and many fall into their hands clothed that are glad when they are escaped naked. Walk not there too late.'

Hackney, a long, scattered village, is chiefly noted for the residence of Edward de Vere, 17th Earl of Oxford, the son-in-law of Lord Burghley, a valiant jouster, a talented poet, a murderous duellist and a wastrel. More likely to be remembered as the man who introduced from Italy the fashion for embroidered and perfumed gloves than for his supposed attempts to write plays, de Vere has now retired from Court.

Highgate, at the top of a steep hill, has several ponds at which you may refresh a tired horse after the climb. Local legend attributes the making of the ponds to a hermit who, as a self-imposed penance, dug them out for gravel to repair the road to Islington. Norden has declared Highgate 'a most pleasant dwelling, yet not so pleasant as healthful', with 'sweet salutary Air'.

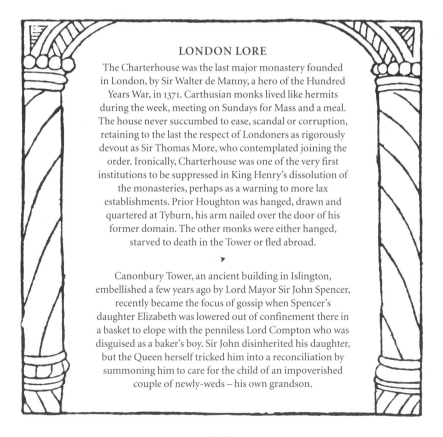

## LONDON LORE

The Charterhouse was the last major monastery founded in London, by Sir Walter de Manny, a hero of the Hundred Years War, in 1371. Carthusian monks lived like hermits during the week, meeting on Sundays for Mass and a meal. The house never succumbed to ease, scandal or corruption, retaining to the last the respect of Londoners as rigorously devout as Sir Thomas More, who contemplated joining the order. Ironically, Charterhouse was one of the very first institutions to be suppressed in King Henry's dissolution of the monasteries, perhaps as a warning to more lax establishments. Prior Houghton was hanged, drawn and quartered at Tyburn, his arm nailed over the door of his former domain. The other monks were either hanged, starved to death in the Tower or fled abroad.

Canonbury Tower, an ancient building in Islington, embellished a few years ago by Lord Mayor Sir John Spencer, recently became the focus of gossip when Spencer's daughter Elizabeth was lowered out of confinement there in a basket to elope with the penniless Lord Compton who was disguised as a baker's boy. Sir John disinherited his daughter, but the Queen herself tricked him into a reconciliation by summoning him to care for the child of an impoverished couple of newly-weds – his own grandson.

Beyond Highgate at Hampstead the great beacon, lit as a warning of invasion at the time of the Spanish Armada, reminds the thoughtful traveller of a turning-point in the nation's history. You can also climb an elm tree so massive that it has steps carved inside it, enabling visitors to admire the view down over London.

Upstream to the west of London stands riverside Chelsea, a village of palaces, once favoured by Henry VIII and Sir Thomas More and latterly the home of the Earl of Shrewsbury, the Duke of Norfolk and the Lord High Admiral. Beyond that, at Fulham, the Bishop of London has his main summer palace. You could be forgiven for thinking it was a college, being built around a quadrangle, fashionably patterned in diaper-work of red and purple bricks and entered via a battlemented tower gatehouse. It is celebrated for the size and excellence of its fruit and kitchen garden.

Upstream further still, but easily reached by boat, is Brentford, a rural, riverside village well known to Londoners as 'a place of resort', by which they mean that it has several inns, like The Three Pigeons, where a man and a woman, looking to enjoy each other's company, can be sure of comfort, cleanliness and discretion.

WHIRLPOOL: *We'll take a coach and rise to Ham or so.*
TENTERHOOK: *O fie upon't, a coach − I cannot abide to be jolted.*

MABEL: *Yet most of your citizens' wives love jolting!*
GOZLIN: *What say you to Blackwall or Limehouse?*
JUDITH: *Every room there smells too much of tar.*
LINSTOCK: *Let's to mine host Dogbolt's at Brainford, then. There you are out of eyes, out of ears; private rooms, sweet linen, winking attendance, and what cheer you will!*
ALL: *Content! To Brainford!*
MABEL: *Ay, ay, let's go by water.*

DEKKER AND THOMAS WEBSTER
WESTWARD HO! ACT II SCENE II

On the south bank of the river, upstream of the old palace of Westminster, Lambeth Palace has been for four centuries the London residence of the Archbishops of Canterbury. You might like to get there on the ferry for horses which crosses the river here and provides the primate with an income from its tolls. Three times a week you can watch a dole being distributed to the poor at the great gateway of the palace. The rest of Lambeth is mostly marsh and market gardens. Downstream of this lies Southwark, the only substantially built-up part of London south of the Thames. Beyond Southwark and to the southeast, the wind-swept plateau of Blackheath is notorious for highway robbery. Twelve miles to the south, in the village of Croydon, the Archbishop of Canterbury has another palace. In the surrounding area walnut trees are found in extraordinary abundance.

## LONDON'S LIFELINES

Travelling through the shires around London will also show the observant traveller where the necessities of the city are drawn from. Surrey's sandy soil does not suit intensive horticulture so its people have become very skilled in managing their woodlands, supplying London with kindling and firing for the hearth, timbers and laths for building, wicker for baskets etc. In the part of Middlesex west of London one of the finest tracts of wheat in the whole country runs from Heston near Hounslow, northwards to Harrow-on-the-Hill and then on to Pinner. The Queen's own bread is only ever made from Heston wheat. Hertfordshire to the north of London supplies barley for brewing beer. At Barnet on Mondays dealers meet for a weekly horse fair, a good opportunity to appraise horse-flesh for free if that is one of your interests.

Norden reserves special praise for Essex, to the east: 'most fat, fruitful and full of profitable things, exceeding (as far as I can find) any other shire for the general commodities and planting ... the English Goshen, the fattest of the land: comparable to Palestina that flowed with milk and honey.' The parts nearest London are great producers of milk, butter and cheese, northwards are hops and corn and wool of the finest quality. Around Ongar, only 20 miles from Whitehall, the thick woods teem with red and fallow deer. Norden has, however, one caution for the traveller: 'But I cannot commend the healthfulness of it, and especially near the sea coast ... and other low places about the creeks, which gave me a most cruel quartan fever.' This hazard discourages the casual visitor and may explain, at least in part, why lonely inlets along the Essex coast are so much favoured by smugglers.

## GREAT HOUSES

### THEOBALDS

Theobalds was built as a country retreat near Cheshunt in Hertfordshire, an easy day's ride north of London and figuring therefore on the itinerary of most foreign visitors. The Queen has been entertained there on at least 12 occasions. In plan it has been arranged as a succession of five courtyards over a quarter of a mile long, making it the second largest house in England after Hampton Court. Five galleries have been added for the Queen to take her exercise whenever cold or rain keeps her from going out.

The Duke of Württemberg has noted that Theobald's is adorned with 'very

> *My house at Theobalds was begun by me with a mean measure but increased by occasion of Her Majesty's often coming, whom to please I never would omit to strain myself to more charges than building it.*
> WILLIAM CECIL, LORD BURGHLEY

GREENWICH.

*Belle Vue. Greenwich affords a splendid prospect across the valley in which London lies.*

artistic paintings and correct landscapes of all the most important and remarkable towns in Christendom', despite the fact that Lord Burghley wasn't actually much interested in paintings, much preferring sculptures. The Green Gallery, over 100 ft long, features representations of the counties of England with the coats of arms of their noblemen and gentry and depictions of local specialities in the way of produce or livestock, such as 'oats and great-bodied beeves' in Lancashire, 'beech trees' for making tools in Buckinghamshire and iron-founding in Sussex. On the roof of the house, one may view the stars and other heavenly bodies by night from the 'Astronomer's Walk'. The roof was originally made flat so that the Queen could stroll there in fine weather. In all Lord Burghley has spent some £25,000 on this house.

The grounds, including no less than four gardens, are well worth seeing even when they close the house to visitors. Lord Burghley's consultant gardener was John Gerard, author of the famous *Herbal*. Around the Great Garden of two acres runs, not a wall, but a canal. Inside you can get lost in a labyrinth or

a maze, be dazzled by a fountain of purest white marble, admire the perspectives from an artificial mount, visit a summer house with marble statues of 12 Roman emperors, fish in a specially stocked pond, row a boat on the lake or be enchanted by the manoeuvres of a fully rigged miniature ship.

### GREENWICH

*We saw many fine objects, amongst them a very costly backgammon set, gift of Christian, Elector of Saxony to the queen. We were then shown a fine high silver-gilt escritoire … [a] saltcellar in the shape of a native … On the side-board was a long cover worked in silver and gold showing the queen in a coach … an exceedingly lovely cover of peacock's feathers sewn together … a rich gilt clock … two fine large globes of heaven and earth … all … gifts to the queen from great potentates.*

THOMAS PLATTER
*TRAVELS IN ENGLAND* • 1599

Greenwich lies five miles downstream from the Tower of London and is the favourite residence of the Queen, as it was of her father. Both of them were born there. The walled park at the rear of the palace has its own herd of deer, where the monarch may both

## LONDON LORE

Queen Catherine of Aragon was kept a virtual prisoner at Greenwich from 1529 to 1531 for refusing to accept that her marriage of 20 years to King Henry had been invalid all along. Perhaps this humiliation of her blameless mother explains why Queen Mary never liked Greenwich and rarely went there. On one of the few occasions that she did, a salute of great guns was fired to welcome her and a cannon ball came right through the wall of her apartment 'to the great terror of herself and her ladies'.

hunt and hawk. The front of the palace gives directly onto the river so that its constant flow of shipping permanently enlivens the scene. Once known as Placentia – the pleasant place – Greenwich was greatly enlarged by Henry VIII, who added a tiltyard and a banqueting hall. He also established a works for the manufacture of armour, staffed by German metalworkers.

### DEPTFORD

Coming from London, just before reaching Greenwich, one comes to the thriving industrial village of Deptford, where Henry VIII established the King's Yard, to build and repair ships for the Royal Navy. You can also visit another royal dockyard nearby at Woolwich.

### RICHMOND PALACE

This riverside palace upstream of London was built by the Queen's grandfather, Henry VII, on the site of a former royal residence, known as Sheen, which was destroyed by fire. He renamed it Richmond after his earldom in Yorkshire and established the first royal library there. In the great hall are 11 life-size statues of the most famous of England's kings and in the chapel a parallel series of kings renowned for their piety. These evidences of princely patronage give the lie to those who said he was a miser.

The Great Orchard supplies provender for the palace kitchens. The Privy Orchard and Garden are surrounded by timber-framed galleries with alcoves for playing chess, dice, tables and cards. There are also bowling alleys, archery butts and tennis courts. As the Queen often keeps court here in the summer, many of her courtiers own houses nearby so that they can be in attendance.

### HAMPTON COURT

*We were led into two chambers, called the presence, or chambers of audience, which shone with tapestry of gold and silver and silk … under the canopy of state are the words embroidered in pearl, vivat Henricus Octavus ['Long Live Henry VIII']. Here is besides a small chapel, richly hung with tapestry, where the Queen performs her devotions … All the other rooms, being very numerous, are adorned with tapestry of gold, silver and velvet ... cushions ornamented with gold and silver ... counterpanes and coverlids of beds lined with ermine: in short all the walls of the palace shine with gold and silver.*

PAUL HENTZNER
TRAVELS IN ENGLAND • 1598

Hampton Court was begun by Henry VIII's chief minister, Cardinal Wolsey, in 1514.

There was already an existing courtyard house on the site, with a moat. Wolsey immediately added a long gallery and extensive kitchens, stables, store-houses etc. so that he could entertain large numbers of visitors, especially the king and his entourage. As proof of the Cardinal's determination to spare no expense in combining magnificence with comfort, water was piped to the site from Combe Hill,

*Go with the flow. The river journey to Hampton Court takes several hours, even when travelling with the tide.*

three miles away, passing in pipes of lead – not leaky elm – through the village of Surbiton and *under* both the Hogsmill and the Thames. The Cardinal then added a second courtyard with a majestic set of royal lodgings, approached by a processional staircase. An Italian master, Giovanni da Maiano, was commissioned to decorate the new courtyard with terracotta roundels depicting Roman emperors. A German artist, Erhard Schon, designed the stained-glass windows of a new chapel. A Venetian ambassador reckoned that the plate on view on the sideboard in the banqueting hall was worth £25,000, and estimated that in total the plate in the house was worth six times that much. Wolsey's collection of 600 tapestries was almost certainly even greater than that of the king. The king was himself clearly impressed and visited Hampton Court on no fewer than 16 separate occasions.

In 1525, Wolsey, sensitive to royal jealousy and anticipating an explosion of

royal ire, tactfully presented Hampton Court to the king. In fairness to His Majesty, Wolsey was allowed to keep on a suite of rooms and was assigned for his own use part of the palace of Richmond. Henry immediately set about a massive programme of enlargement. By the time the French ambassador saw the palace in 1527 it had 280 rooms. In 1540 Nicholas Oursian installed an astounding clock which showed the hour, day and month, phases of the moon, signs of the zodiac and time of high water at London Bridge. By the time of his death Henry VIII had spent £62,000 on Hampton Court, making it the largest of all the royal residences outside London itself.

The Queen sometimes spends Christmas at Hampton Court on account of its size, which gives plenty of room for festivities, but she dislikes the place, perhaps because, a few years after her accession, she nearly died of the smallpox here, an event which is never referred to in her presence.

Thomas Platter, on his recent visit to Hampton Court, much admired the 'maze ... and two marble fountains ... should one miss one's way, not only are taste, vision and smell delighted, but the gladsome birdsongs and plashing fountains please the ear; indeed, it is like an earthly paradise.'

*Built with so great sumptousness and rare workmanship, that it aspireth to the very top of ostentation for show; so as a man may think, that all the skill of Architecture is in this piece of work bestowed, and heaped up together. So many statues and lively images, so many wonders ... and works seeming to contend with Roman antiquities, that most worthily it may have and maintain still this name that it hath of Nonsuch.*

WILLIAM CAMDEN
BRITANNIA • 1586

## NONSUCH PALACE

Nonsuch Palace lies near Ewell in the county of Surrey, an hour's ride from Hampton Court. It was built by Henry VIII as a hunting lodge and for entertaining, or rather, impressing, foreign visitors. As its name proclaims, it was meant that there should be none other like it.

There is no other royal residence that so clearly expresses the power of a monarch. The site was previously occupied by the village of Cuddington which was razed to the ground, parish church and all. A thousand acres of land was purchased, against the wishes of the owners, and walled in. Several highways were diverted. The foundations of the palace were made from the stones of the dissolved priory of Merton, situated nearby. Expert craftsmen were recruited from abroad to do the actual work of building and decoration under the direction of two Italian masters, John of Padua and Antonio Toto dell' Annunziata of Florence.

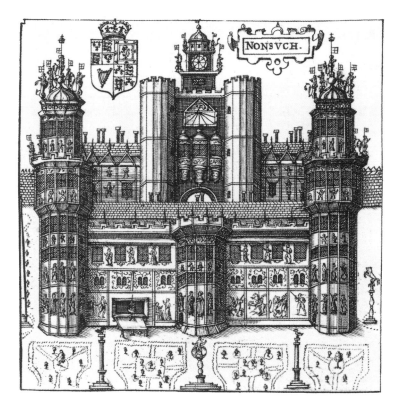

NONSVCH.

Unlike Hampton Court, Nonsuch does not aim to overawe the onlooker by its sheer size. It stands only two storeys high, enclosing two courtyards. This makes it, as palaces go, quite modest in scale. But its décor is both exuberant and exquisite, the skyline a forest of chimneys, turrets, pinnacles, cupolas and battlements, the façade festooned with plasterwork, panelling, plaques and portraits, the landscaped grounds dotted with fountains, statuary, columns, obelisks, an archway, a pyramid, a banqueting house and the

*To Let? Owning 50 palaces Henry VIII never actually found time to live at Nonsuch.*

first grotto ever made in England. Ironically the king only ever spent four days at Nonsuch and it was still unfinished at his death, ten years after the project was started. Queen Mary sold it to the Earl of Arundel, who frequently entertained the present Queen there for hunting. His heir has recently sold it back to her. Her Majesty has never built a new palace – but she is not averse to acquiring them.

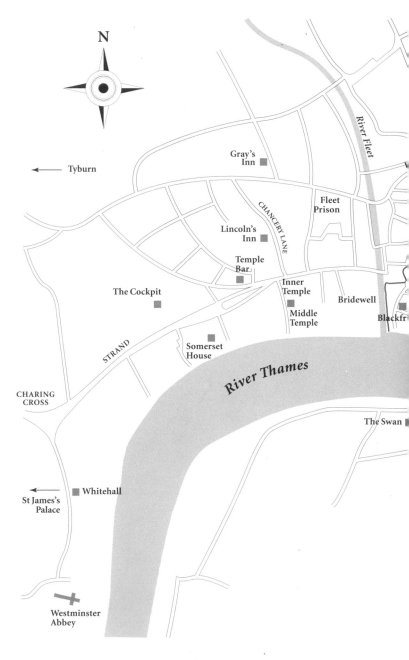

N

Tyburn →

Gray's
Inn

River Fleet

CHANCERY LANE

Fleet
Prison

Lincoln's
Inn

Temple
Bar

The Cockpit

Inner
Temple

Bridewell

Middle
Temple

Blackfr

STRAND

Somerset
House

River Thames

CHARING
CROSS

The Swan

← Whitehall

St James's
Palace

Westminster
Abbey

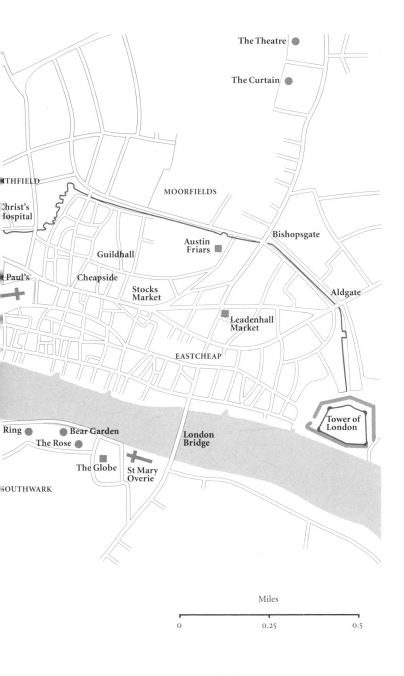

The Theatre

The Curtain

THFIELD

MOORFIELDS

hrist's
Hospital

Bishopsgate

Austin
Friars

Guildhall

Paul's

Cheapside

Stocks
Market

Aldgate

Leadenhall
Market

EASTCHEAP

Tower of
London

Ring

Bear Garden

The Rose

London
Bridge

The Globe

St Mary
Overie

SOUTHWARK

Miles

0          0.25          0.5

# AUTHOR'S NOTE

The setting for this guide is London in 1599/1600. I have tried to keep the material included as consistent as possible with this date. I would like to thank my friends Michael Berlin of Birkbeck College for bibliographic advice and John Richardson of Historical Publications for the use of books from his extensive London collection. At Thames & Hudson, Colin Ridler for his remarkable patience and tact, Sophie Mackinder for the professionalism and enthusiasm of her support, Karin Fremer for her design, Alice Foster and Sally Paley for their picture research and Celia Falconer. Finally my wife, Sheila, for her forbearance, and daughters Victoria and Elena for their inspiration and interruptions.

# SOURCE OF ILLUSTRATIONS

Private Collection 19, 91, 143
From *Psalms*, 1563 36
From Roxburghe Ballads 14, 25, 27, 64, 66
From Roxburghe Ballads. British Library, London 100, 128
Title page from Edmund Spenser, *The Faerie Queene*, 1590 18
Title page from John Stow, *A Survay of London*, 1598 8
Sudeley Castle, Winchcombe 17
From George Turbevile, *Book of Hunting*, 1575 57, 130
Victoria & Albert Museum, London 80, 127
From J.C. Visscher, *View of London*, 1616 94
Walker Art Gallery, National Museums Liverpool. Photo Bridgeman Art Library, London 6 and throughout
Westminster School, London 7b

COLOUR PLATE SECTION
National Portrait Gallery, London I
Private Collection II
The Right Hon. Earl of Derby. Photo Bridgeman Art Library, London III
Parham Park, Pulborough IV
National Portrait Gallery, London V
The Marquess of Bath, Longleat House, Warminster VI
Glasgow University Library. Photo Bridgeman Art Library, London VII
Trustees of the late Countess Beauchamp VIII
National Portrait Gallery, London IX
Society of Antiquaries of London X
From *Civitatis Orbis Terrarum*, c.1574. Folger Shakespeare Library, Washington D.C. XI
Paul Mellon Collection, Yale Center for British Art, New Haven. Photo Bridgeman Art Library, London XII
Edinburgh University Library XIII
British Museum, London XIV
Private Collection XV
Fitzwilliam Museum, Cambridge XVI

# INDEX

First published in 2009 in paperback in the United States of America by Thames & Hudson Inc., 500 Fifth Avenue, New York, New York 10110

thamesandhudsonusa.com

Library of Congress Catalog Card Number 2008908226

ISBN 978-0-500-28793-4

Printed and bound in China by SNP Leefung Printers Limited